THE XXL AIR FRYER COOKBOOK UK 2023

Quick, Healthy & Super-Delicious Air Fryer Recipes for Family & Friends I Everyday Enjoyment for Beginner & Advanced Users I Breakfast, Dinner, Sweet Treats & More

WILLIAM R. GARDNER

ISBN - 9798371708694

TABLE OF CONTENTS

EXCLUSIVE BONUS

40 Weight Loss Recipes

&

14 Days Meal Plan

Scan the QR-Code and receive
the FREE download:

Welcome to Your Easy-To-Learn
Air Fryer Recipe Guide

Welcome to your easy-to-learn air fryer recipe guide - the only cookbook that any air fryer owner needs to use!

This is the perfect cookbook for those of you who just getting started in the world of food and cooking. All you need is an air fryer and you'll be able to create every recipe in this book. Even if you're an avid cook already, you'll enjoy browsing these recipes and adding your own unique spin to traditional, classic dishes.

Inside this cookbook, you'll learn:
- What an air fryer is
- Where air fryers began and how they have developed over the years
- The various types of air fryers
- The best foods and dishes to create in an air fryer
- The best air fryers on the market and which brands are reliable
- How to use an air fryer
- The benefits of cooking in an air fryer

All of this information is followed up with a wide range of different recipes for you to try using your handy air fryer. You'll find recipes for all meals of the day, including breakfast, lunch, dinner, desserts, and snacks. The whole family can enjoy a delicious range of exciting dishes for years to come!

We've included the nutritional values per serving (including calories, carbs, protein, and fats) for every dish so that you can track your calorie or macronutrient intake more easily. We've also added the total preparation and cooking times so that you can plan your meals around your busy schedule.

So, are you ready to get started? Grab your air fryer and let's get cooking!

What is an Air Fryer and Why is it Better Than a Deep Fryer?

Air fryers are similar to ovens. You can use this handy kitchen gadget to cook a wide range of foods, dishes, and desserts.

Air fryers use specialised heating elements that are usually placed at the top of the machine to heat the food inside. A large fan inside the machine helps to circulate the hot air around the air fryer basket via convection to increase the efficiency of the cooking process. Unlike many other cooking gadgets, air fryers are able to cook ingredients in such a way that they become extra crispy and delicious.

A lot of people get confused between deep fryers and air fryers because they look and sound like very similar pieces of machinery. However, there are key differences that make the air fryer superior to the deep fryer.

Unlike deep fryers which require a large amount of hot oil to cook your dishes, air fryers require absolutely no oil at all. Instead of using hot oil to heat your food, they use heating elements and a large convection fan to cook the ingredients all the way through.

Deep fryers also take longer to cook your food and require more energy to do so because there is a pre-heating phase. Air fryers don't need to be pre-heated and you can add your ingredients to the basket inside the machine and get started with your cooking immediately. They are, therefore, much better when you're a busy person who doesn't want to spend hours in the kitchen after work!

If you use an air fryer, you also achieve the same batter-style coating that you get with a deep fryer but your dish will be a lot healthier and you will still have a crispy dish by the end of the cooking process.

Where Did Air Fryers Begin and How Have They Developed Over the Years?

The air fryer was patented by Philips Electronic Company a while back. The patent describes the kitchen appliance that is used as a healthier alternative to deep frying by using hot air and little or no oil.

The main reason why people choose to use an air fryer over other methods of cooking is that they require a lot less oil than deep frying.

They're also much quicker at cooking lots of food than an oven due to the close proximity of the heating elements to the ingredients that are being cooked and the powerful fan aiding the cooking process. You can get a healthier meal in a shorter amount of time, and that's enough to make anybody fall in love with the amazing air fryer.

We will talk more about the many benefits of using an air fryer over other cooking techniques further on in this book. First, we will quickly cover the key differences between the air fryer and the deep fryer because many people get confused between the two.

What Are the Different Types of Air Fryers?

There are two main types of air fryers that you can buy nowadays – basket air fryers and air fryer ovens. Both are great options but they differ slightly, so it's important to know which one is best for you.

Basket air fryers have a removable basket that holds your ingredients. Hot air circulates around the air fryer to cook the food within minutes. The removable basket makes it easy to get your ingredients out of the machine when they're ready. This type of air fryer is a user-friendly option for those of you who aren't the most confident in the kitchen.

Air fryer ovens are designed to be very similar to toaster ovens or convection ovens. They often have several functions, so they can cook your ingredients in a number of ways, such as baking, grilling, frying, and broiling. Ultimately, they are multi-purpose or multifunctional kitchen gadgets.

How Do You Use An Air Fryer?

Every air fryer comes with a detailed instruction manual that will tell you about all of the different settings that the air fryer has and the function of each button. You can keep the instruction manual close when you are using the air fryer to refer to when you're cooking if you're unsure how to operate the machine properly.

Although every air fryer is unique and will have different settings based on the manufacturer and the model of your machine. However, we've detailed a general set of guidelines that will apply to pretty much every air fryer.

1. Gather your ingredients and follow your recipe book up until the point where it tells you to place the ingredients in your air fryer.

2. Before you start making your recipe, like the mesh basket of the air fryer with baking sheets.

3. When you reach this stage in your recipe, put your ingredients in the lined mesh basket. Be careful not to overfill the basket, as this might affect the way the food cooks and reduce the crispiness of your dish.

4. If you're cooking meat or vegetables and you want them to be extra crispy, add a small coating of oil to the ingredients before placing them in the air fryer.

5. Close the lid of the air fryer and choose your setting and temperature. Most air fryers have pre-set times and temperatures that you can choose from to get the perfect crispiness of your dish. Most machines offer cooking times between 5 to 30 minutes and temperature settings between 180 and 250 degrees Celsius.

6. Allow the air fryer to do its thing. You can now relax and wait for your ingredients to cook. When your food is ready, you can enjoy your delicious dish.

What Dishes Can You Make in an Air Fryer?

There is a wide variety of dishes that you can create in an air fryer, including meats, fish, tofu, carbohydrates, and vegetables.

For some ingredients, you may need to add a little bit of oil to ensure they cook properly and come out of the machine extra crispy. However, if you marinate your ingredients in a lot of sauce, you might not need to add any oil. The details of this would be specified in the recipe that you're following.

Generally, it's better to use vegetable oil instead of butter when you're cooking foods in an air fryer. Oil has a lower melting point, meaning it heats up much more quickly than butter does, so you won't need to wait as long for your ingredients to fully cook. Every recipe in this book uses olive oil but almost any plant-based oil will be suitable for your air fryer.

Popular ingredients that you'll find in lots of different air fryer recipes both in this book and online include:

1. Meat – poultry, pork, beef, turkey
2. Seafood – fish, scallops, shrimps, seaweed
3. Grains – pasta, rice, noodles, buckwheat, cous cous
4. Starchy vegetables – potatoes, swede, parsnips, turnips
5. Non-starchy vegetables – broccoli, kale, carrots, sprouts, beetroot, peas, sweetcorn
6. Meat alternatives – tofu, tempeh, soy products

What Are the Best Air Fryers on the Market?

There are hundreds of different air fryer brands out there, all of which offer a variety of different models and versions of similar machines. When you're searching for a new air fryer, make sure to read closely about each brand's unique features and offerings so that you can find the best one for your needs and wants.

Here are some of our top recommendations to consider when you're buying a brand-new air fryer for your kitchen

1. Black and Decker Purify Air Fryer
2. Breville Halo Rotisserie Air Fryer Oven
3. Cosori Air Fryer
4. Cosori Dual Blaze 6.4L Smart Air Fryer
5. Cuisinart Air Fryer Mini Oven
6. Instant Vortex Plus Dual Air Fryer
7. Magic Bullet 2.5-litre Air Fryer
8. Ninja Air Fryer Max
9. Ninja Foodi MAX 14-in-1 SmartLid Air Fryer
10. Philips Avance Turbo-Star Air Fryer
11. PowerXL Vortex Air Fryer
12. Sage the Smart Oven Air Fryer
13. Salter Dual Cook Pro 8.2L Air Fryer
14. Tefal ActiFry Genius 2-in-1 Air Fryer
15. Tower T17023 Air Fryer

How Do You Use an Air Fryer?

Every air fryer that you come across will have an instruction manual included in the box. You can use this if needed when you're cooking in the kitchen.

Although each air fryer manufacturer will create products that have unique features, functions, and settings. Take a little bit of when you first buy your air fryer to familiarise yourself with the specific functions of the device.

Below, we've included a few general steps that you can follow when using an air fryer of any kind.

1. Follow the recipe accordingly until you reach the stage at which you're adding the ingredients into the air fryer.

2. Open the air fryer and add the foods into the mesh basket (lined or unlined, depending on the recipe that you're using).

3. Depending on the size of the air fryer you've chosen, you'll be able to add up to a certain volume of food to avoid overfilling the basket. Overfilling the basket will cause the food to be undercooked in certain parts.

4. Add a drizzle of olive oil if you're using it.

5. Choose your cooking temperature or time or choose a specific cooking setting if your air fryer has this option. With a lot of air fryers, the time settings range from between 5 and 30 minutes, and the temperature options are between 180 and 250 degrees Celsius.

6. When you've added your ingredients, shut the lid of the air fryer, and chosen your cooking settings, leave the machine to do its thing.

7. Once your dish is cooked, carefully take it out of the air fryer and serve.

8. Allow the air fryer to cool down before you wipe it clean to avoid burning yourself.

9. When you're cleaning the air fryer, always use a soft cloth and warm water. Wipe off any leftover bits of food and take out the basket to wash in the dishwasher or sink.

10. You should wash your air fryer after every use.

What Are the Benefits of Using an Air Fryer?

There are lots of benefits to having an air fryer in your kitchen and we've covered some of the main benefits below:

1. No preheating is required - when you're using an air fryer, you don't need to wait for the elements to heat up before adding your ingredients, so you can get cooking as quickly as possible. Even if you use oil, it will still take a lot less time to cook your food than if you were using other cooking appliances, such as a slow cooker or a traditional oven.

2. No oil is required – you don't need to add any oil at all when you're using an air fryer. This makes your dishes healthier and less oily, but just as tasty.

3. Less time and energy cooking each day - there is no preheating time required, so you can cut down the time that you spend in the kitchen cooking your meals and snacks significantly.

4. Crispy food - the hot air can circulate around your food efficiently thanks to the large fan inside the air fryer, giving you a cooked and crispy dish in no time.

5. You can cook a variety of dishes in the air fryer – they're a great kitchen device for those of you following a vegetarian, vegan, paleo, pescetarian, or keto diet because there is such a wide variety of dishes that you can cook in an air fryer.

6. Air fryers are safe to use - you don't need to worry about getting splashed with oil or hot food with the air fryer because the lid is kept shut during the entire cooking process.

7. Air fryers are easy to clean – with a quick wipe down, your air fryer is ready for its next use.

8. Sleek and stylish – every modern-day air fryer looks great. They have premium designs that fit perfectly into any kitchen aesthetic.

9. They take up very little room in the kitchen - air fryers are compact and can easily fit into your kitchen cupboard if you want to store them out of sight.

10. Easy to transport – air fryers are usually light ad easily portable, so you can move them around your kitchen easily.

EXCLUSIVE BONUS

40 Weight Loss Recipes

&

14 Days Meal Plan

Scan the QR-Code and receive
the FREE download:

Recipes

Now you've learned everything you need to know about air fryers, it's time to start creating your very own delicious dishes at home. Below, you will find recipes covering all mealtimes, including breakfast, lunch, dinner, and snacks. You can enjoy these dishes by yourself or with your friends and family members.

BREAKFAST

If you're using your air fryer to prepare breakfast, you won't need to organize your ingredients or switch your device on the night before. You can roll out of bed and prepare and cook your breakfast in the air fryer within 10 minutes! However, if you have some spare time in the mornings before you start your day, you can try a more complex air fryer recipe.

We've included a range of different recipes that you can create for a delicious and healthy breakfast using your air fryer below. Regardless of your preferences and your lifestyle, there is a breakfast recipe (or several!) for everybody below, so keep reading!

Savoury Air Fryer Cheese Croissants

MAKES 4 SERVINGS
PREPARATION TIME - 10 MINUTES
COOKING TIME - 10 MINUTES
NUTRITIONAL VALUES PER SERVING - 212 KCALS, 18 G CARBS, 7 G PROTEIN, 14 G FAT

INGREDIENTS

- 4 pre-packaged croissants
- 100 g feta cheese, crumbled
- 1 tsp dried mixed herbs
- 1 tsp garlic powder
- ½ tsp black pepper

METHOD

1. Preheat the air fryer to 180 degrees Celsius. Line the inner mesh basket with parchment paper.
2. Cut the croissants evenly in half and lay each half out on a clean surface.
3. In a bowl, combine the crumbled feta cheese, dried herbs, garlic powder, and black pepper.
4. Spoon the mixture evenly onto one half of each of the four croissants and cover with the second half of each croissant to seal the filling inside.
5. Transfer the croissants into the lined air fryer basket, shut the lid, and cook for 10 minutes until the pastry is golden and crispy, and the feta cheese has melted.

Air Fryer Apple and Cinnamon Pastry Turnovers

MAKES 12 SERVINGS
PREPARATION TIME - 15 MINUTES
COOKING TIME - 10 MINUTES
NUTRITIONAL VALUE PER SERVING - 198 CALORIES, 29 G
CARBOHYDRATES, 4 G FAT, 5 G PROTEIN

INGREDIENTS

FOR THE CINNAMON APPLES:

- 4 apples
- 1 tsp cinnamon
- 1 tsp maple syrup

FOR THE TURNOVERS:

- 1 sheet of frozen puff pastry
- 1 egg, beaten

METHOD

1. Peel and dice the apples, and place them in a bowl. Add the cinnamon and maple syrup to the bowl and toss to fully coat the apples.
2. Lay the puff pastry sheet out flat on a clean surface and gently brush it with the beaten egg.
3. Cut the puff pastry into 4 equal squares and spoon the apple mixture evenly into the centre of each. Told the pastry to conceal the apple inside and use a fork or your fingers to press the corners and edges securely down.
4. Transfer the apple turnovers to the air fryer basket and cook for 15 minutes at 180 degree Celsius until golden and crispy.
5. Serve while hot with some cream or ice cream.

Air Fryer All-Day Breakfast

MAKES 2 SERVINGS
PREPARATION TIME - 10 MINUTES
COOKING TIME - 10 MINUTES
NUTRITIONAL VALUE PER SERVING - 659 KCALS, 41 G CARBS, 43 G PROTEIN, 40 G FAT

INGREDIENTS

- 4 sausages
- 8 rashers of bacon
- 1 x 400g can of chopped tomatoes
- 1 x 400g baked beans
- 4 eggs, beaten
- 200g button mushrooms
- 2 tsp butter

METHOD

1. Place the sausages and bacon around the edges of the air fryer, making sure they aren't stuck together or touching.
2. Add the remaining ingredients to the air fryer and give everything a good stir.
3. Switch the air fryer to a heat of around 200 degrees Celsius, close the lid, and allow it to cook for 10 minutes.
4. Once all of the ingredients are cooked, turn the air fryer off and serve your all-day breakfast with a coffee or glass of fruit juice.

Air Fryer Peanut Butter Oatmeal

MAKES 4 SERVINGS
PREPARATION TIME - 5 MINUTES
COOKING TIME - 5 MINUTES
NUTRITIONAL VALUE PER SERVING - 212 KCALS, 30 G CARBS, 10 G PROTEIN, 6 G FAT

INGREDIENTS

- 200 g classic rolled oats
- 500 ml water
- 500 ml oat milk

- 2 tbsp smooth peanut butter
- 2 tbsp chia seeds

METHOD

1. In a bowl, add the rolled oats, water, oat milk, peanut butter, and chia seeds. Stir until they form a smooth and consistent mixture.
2. Transfer the mixture to the air fryer, shut the lid, and cook at 180 degrees Celsius.
3. Serve the oatmeal with a topping of your choice. You might want some fresh banana and strawberry slices, a sprinkle of cinnamon, or an extra dollop of peanut butter.

Air Fryer Berry and Banana Granola

MAKES 8 SERVINGS
PREPARATION TIME - 5 MINUTES
COOKING TIME - 10 MINUTES
NUTRITIONAL VALUE PER SERVING - 154 KCALS, 18 G CARBS, 8 G PROTEIN, 5 G FAT

INGREDIENTS

- 100 g raw and unsalted mixed nuts (peanuts, cashews, and walnuts)
- 100 g raw and unsalted mixed seeds (pumpkin, sunflower, and chia)
- 100 g dried berries
- 100 g dried banana chips, chopped into small pieces
- 400 g rolled oats
- 100 g unsweetened coconut flakes
- 2 tsp cinnamon
- 1 tsp nutmeg
- 2 tbsp coconut oil or olive oil
- 4 tbsp honey or agave syrup
- 1 tbsp vanilla extract

METHOD

1. In a large mixing bowl, combine the mixed nuts, mixed seeds, dried berries, dried banana chips, rolled oats, coconut flakes, cinnamon, and nutmeg. Mix well.

2. Add the coconut oil or olive oil, honey or agave syrup, and vanilla extract. Toss to coat all of the ingredients until they begin to form small clumps.

3. Transfer the mixture to the air fryer and close the lid. Cook the granola for 8-10 minutes at 200 degrees Celsius until the oats are golden and crispy.

4. Serve the granola for breakfast on top of some yogurt or with some milk. Store any leftovers in an airtight jar for a maximum of 5 days

Air Fryer Egg and Edam Souffles

MAKES 4 SERVINGS
PREPARATION TIME - 5 MINUTES
COOKING TIME - 10 MINUTES
NUTRITIONAL VALUES PER SERVING - 156 KCALS, 12 G CARBS, 10 G PROTEIN, 6 G FAT

INGREDIENTS

- 8 eggs
- 100 g fresh spinach
- 50 g Edam cheese, grated
- 1 tsp black pepper
- 1 tsp salt

METHOD

1. Preheat the air fryer to 200 degrees Celsius. Line an 8-pan muffin tray with parchment paper or grease with olive oil.
2. Whisk the eggs in a bowl and stir in the spinach. Press into the bottom of each lined muffin cup.
3. Top with the grated cheese and a sprinkle of black pepper and black pepper.
4. Place the muffin tray into the lined air fryer basket, close the lid, and cook the egg, spinach, and Edam souffles for 10 minutes until the eggs are set and the cheese is fully melted.
5. Serve the souffles while they are hot for breakfast.

Air Fryer Sausage, Egg, and Cheese

MAKES 8 SERVINGS
PREPARATION TIME - 10 MINUTES
COOKING TIME - 10 MINUTES
NUTRITIONAL VALUES PER SERVING - 288 KCALS, 14 G CARBS, 9 G PROTEIN, 17 G FAT

INGREDIENTS

- 1 tbsp olive oil
- 8 sausages
- ½ white onion, peeled and sliced
- 12 eggs
- 100 g cheddar cheese, grated
- 1 tbsp butter
- 1 tsp salt
- ½ tsp black pepper

METHOD

1. Preheat the air fryer to 180 degrees Celsius and line the bottom of the basket with greaseproof paper.
2. Heat 1 tbsp of olive oil in a large frying pan and add the sausages and white onion slices. Cook for 5 minutes and transfer to the air fryer basket.
3. In a bowl, combine the cheddar cheese, eggs, butter, salt, and black pepper. Pour into the air fryer basket and shut the lid.
4. Cook for 10 minutes until all of the ingredients are well cooked.
5. Serve the sausage, egg, and cheese while steaming hot.

Air Fryer Eggy Bread

MAKES 2 SERVINGS
PREPARATION TIME - 10 MINUTES
COOKING TIME - 5 MINUTES
NUTRITIONAL VALUES PER SERVING - 243 KCALS, 22 G CARBS, 6 G PROTEIN, 6 G FAT

INGREDIENTS

- 4 slices white bread
- 4 eggs
- 200 ml milk (any type)

- 2 tbsp caster sugar
- 1 tsp ground cinnamon
- 1 tbsp honey

METHOD

1. Cut each slice of bread into 2 even rectangles and set aside.
2. In a bowl, whisk the 4 eggs until well beaten. Stir in the milk, caster sugar, and ground cinnamon.
3. Soak the sliced bread in the eggy mixture until fully covered and transfer to the air fryer.
4. Switch the air fryer onto a heat setting of around 200 degrees Celsius. Shut the lid and cook the eggy bread for 5 minutes.
5. Serve the eggy bread while it's still hot and add a drizzle of maple syrup on top.

Air Fryer Pain au Chocolat

MAKES 4 SERVINGS
PREPARATION TIME - 10 MINUTES
COOKING TIME - 10 MINUTES
NUTRITIONAL VALUES PER SERVING - 234 KCALS, 19 G CARBS, 5 G PROTEIN, 15 G FAT

INGREDIENTS

- 4 croissants
- 100 g milk chocolate chips
- 1 tbsp butter

METHOD

1. Preheat the air fryer to 180 degrees Celsius and line the mesh basket using greaseproof paper.
2. Cut each of the croissants in half lengthways and sprinkle the chocolate chips evenly into the centre of one half of the croissants. Top with the other half of the croissants to seal in the chocolate chip filling.
3. Transfer the croissants to the lined air fryer basket and brush the tops with a little bit of butter.
4. Shut the air fryer lid and cook the croissants for 8-10 minutes until the pastry is crispy and golden, and the chocolate chips inside have melted.

Air Fryer Sausage Breakfast Wraps

MAKES 4 SERVINGS
PREPARATION TIME - 20 MINUTES
COOKING TIME - 20 MINUTES
NUTRITIONAL VALUES PER SERVING - 421 KCALS, 34 G CARBS, 12 G PROTEIN, 14 G FAT

INGREDIENTS

- 1 white potato, chopped
- 2 tbsp olive oil
- 1 tsp salt
- 1 tsp black pepper
- 8 sausages, uncooked
- 4 white or seeded tortillas
- 4 eggs, beaten
- 200 ml milk (any kind)
- 100 g cheddar cheese, grated

METHOD

1. Preheat the air fryer to 200 degrees Celsius and line the air fryer mesh basket with greaseproof paper, olive oil, or butter.
2. Place the white potato in a bowl and drizzle 1 tbsp olive oil, salt, and black pepper over the top. Cook in the air fryer for 5 minutes. Once cooked, set aside.
3. Heat the remaining 1 tbsp olive oil in a frying pan and add the sausages. Cook for 5-7 minutes until slightly browned. Remove the sausages from the pan and set them aside on paper towels to drain.
4. In a bowl, whisk together the beaten eggs and milk, and pour into the hot frying pan. Cook until eggs begin to set and use a fork to scramble them.
5. Add the egg mixture to a bowl, along with the potato, sausages, and cheddar cheese.
6. Lay the tortillas down on an even, clean surface and evenly spoon the egg, potato, sausage, and cheese ingredients into the centre of each. Roll the wraps up tightly. Use toothpicks to keep them together if necessary.
7. Transfer the wraps to the air fryer and cook for 10 minutes until golden and hot, turning them over halfway through.
8. Enjoy the breakfast sausage wraps with a glass of orange juice or a hot coffee!

Air Fryer Chocolate, Peanut Butter, and Banana Toasties

MAKES 2 SERVINGS
PREPARATION TIME - 10 MINUTES
COOKING TIME - 10 MINUTES
NUTRITIONAL VALUES PER SERVING - 350 KCALS, 25 G CARBS, 7 G PROTEIN, 10 G FAT

INGREDIENTS

- 4 slices of bread
- 1 tbsp chocolate hazelnut spread
- 1 tbsp peanut butter
- 2 bananas
- 1 tbsp honey
- 1 tsp cinnamon

METHOD

1. Lay the four slices of bread out flat on a clean surface. Spread the chocolate hazelnut spread onto two slices and peanut butter onto the other two slices.
2. Chop the banana into even pieces and place on top of the two slices of bread with the chocolate hazelnut spread.
3. Sprinkle some cinnamon on top of the banana slices.
4. Place the slices of bread with peanut butter on top of the banana and gently press down to seal in the banana.
5. Transfer the toasties to the air fryer and close the lid. Cook the toasties at 180 degrees Celsius for 10 minutes.
6. Once cooked, remove the toasties and enjoy while hot for breakfast.

Air Fryer Sausage Burritos

MAKES 4 SERVINGS
PREPARATION TIME - 20 MINUTES
COOKING TIME - 5 MINUTES
NUTRITIONAL VALUES PER SERVING - 314 KCALS, 29 G CARBS, 14 G PROTEIN, 14 G FAT

INGREDIENTS

- 2 tbsp butter
- 2 tbsp olive oil
- 4 white tortillas
- 400 g sausage meat, ground (or a vegan alternative)
- 400 g potatoes, peeled and chopped
- 1 red, green, or yellow pepper, deseeded and sliced
- 8 eggs
- 1 tsp black pepper
- ½ tsp salt
- 1 tsp garlic powder
- 1 tsp Italian seasoning
- 100 g cheddar cheese, grated

METHOD

1. Preheat the air fryer to a medium heat setting.
2. Lay the tortillas out on a clean surface.
3. Heat 2 tbsp butter in a large frying pan and add the sausages. Cook for 8-10 minutes until browned.
4. Add the potatoes to the pan and cook for a further 3-4 minutes. Remove from the pan and set aside. Add 2 tbsp olive oil.
5. Heat the olive oil for a few seconds before adding the pepper into the pan and cook for 3-4 minutes until softened. Set aside.
6. Beat the eggs in a bowl and add the black pepper, salt, garlic powder, and Italian seasoning. Add the eggs to the pan and cook for 4-5 minutes until they're slightly cooked, but not fully cooked.
7. Evenly spread the sausages, potatoes, green pepper, and scrambled eggs into the centre of each tortilla. Sprinkle the cheese on top and roll each tortilla up to seal the ingredients inside.
8. Transfer the filled breakfast tortillas to the air fryer basket and cook for 5-6 minutes.
9. Serve the sausage tortillas for breakfast while hot.

Air Fryer Bacon Rolls

MAKES 4 SERVINGS
PREPARATION TIME - 15 MINUTES
COOKING TIME - 5 MINUTES
NUTRITIONAL VALUES PER SERVING - 317 KCALS, 23 G CARBS, 12 G PROTEIN, 16 G FAT

INGREDIENTS

- 2 tbsp olive oil
- 6 strips bacon
- 400 g crescent pastry rolls
- 1 tsp onion powder

METHOD

1. Preheat the air fryer to a medium heat.
2. Heat the olive oil in a frying pan and add the strips of bacon, 2 at a time. Cook for 8-10 minutes until browned and crispy. Set aside on paper towels to drain off the excess oil for a few minutes before cutting into small slices.
3. Unroll the crescent pasty rolls and separate into 8 even triangles. Add a sprinkle of onion powder to each, before adding the chopped bacon. and remaining bacon over triangles.
4. Roll each crescent up to secure the bacon inside. Transfer to the air fryer basket and close the lid. Cook for 8-10 minutes.
5. Eat the rolls while still warm.

Air Fryer Scotch Eggs

MAKES 4 SERVINGS
PREPARATION TIME - 15 MINUTES
COOKING TIME - 15 MINUTES
NUTRITIONAL VALUES PER SERVING - 267 KCALS, 18 G CARBS, 12 G PROTEIN, 11 G FAT

INGREDIENTS

- 500 g pork sausage or vegan sausages
- 1 tsp salt
- 1 tsp black pepper
- 6 hard boiled eggs, plus 1 extra egg, beaten
- 200 g cornflakes, crushed

METHOD

1. Preheat the air fryer to a high setting.
2. Evenly divide the pork sausage or vegan sausages and flatten the meat onto a clean surface. Sprinkle salt and black pepper onto the sausages.
3. Add the hard boiled eggs on top of the flattened sausages and roll the meat around the eggs to form sealed packages.
4. Roll each scotch egg in the beaten egg and cover with crushed cornflakes.
5. Carefully transfer the scotch eggs to the air fryer basket and shut the lid. Cook for 12-15 minutes until hot and cooked. Serve hot or cold.

Air Fryer Sesame Seed Bagels

MAKES 4 SERVINGS
PREPARATION TIME - 20 MINUTES
COOKING TIME - 10 MINUTES
NUTRITIONAL VALUES PER SERVING - 243 KCALS, 25 G CARBS, 9 G PROTEIN, 9 G FAT

INGREDIENTS

- 400 g self-raising flour
- 50 g granulated sugar
- 4 tbsp sesame seeds
- 100 ml Greek yoghurt
- 1 tbsp olive oil
- 1 egg

METHOD

1. Preheat the air fryer to 180 °C degrees Celsius and line the bottom of the basket with parchment paper.
2. In a large mixing bowl, combine the self-raising flour, granulated sugar, and half of the sesame seeds
3. Fold in the Greek yoghurl and olive oil, and stir to fully combine all of the ingredients into a smooth, slightly tacky dough.
4. Roll the dough into 8 equal balls on a clean surface. Press each ball down using the palms of your hands to create even patties that are around 1.5 inches thick.
5. Using your thumb, carefully create holes in the centre of each patty to form bagels.
6. In a bowl, whisk the eggs until fully beaten. Use a pastry brush to lightly coat each bagel in the beaten egg. Press the rest of the sesame seeds into the top of each bagel, being careful not to break them.
7. Transfer the bagels to the air fryer and cook for 8-10 minutes until the bagels are golden and the dough is fully cooked.
8. Place the bagels on a drying rack and leave them to cool for 10 minutes.
9. Serve the bagels hot or cold with a topping of your choice and store leftovers in an airtight container for up to five days.

Air Fryer Apple and Blackberry Bites

MAKES 4 SERVINGS
PREPARATION TIME - 10 MINUTES
COOKING TIME - 10 MINUTES
NUTRITIONAL VALUES PER SERVING - 121 KCALS, 13 G CARBS, 3 G PROTEIN, 3 G FAT

INGREDIENTS

- ♦ 2 apples
- ♦ 100 g fresh blackberries
- ♦ 4 tbsp oats
- ♦ 2 tbsp brown sugar
- ♦ 1 tsp ground cinnamon
- ♦ 2 tsp ground nutmeg

METHOD

1. Preheat the air fryer to 180 °C degrees Celsius and line the bottom of the basket with parchment paper.
2. Wash and peel the apples before cutting them into small cubes.
3. Place the apple chunks into a bowl along with the blackberries, oats, brown sugar, ground cinnamon, and ground nutmeg. Stir well.
4. Spoon the mixture into small balls of a similar size. Transfer the balls into the air fryer basket and close the lid.
5. Cook for 8-10 minutes until the fruit has softened and the bites are crispy on the edges.
6. Eat hot or cold and store any leftovers in the fridge for no more than five days.

Air Fryer Cheese and Egg Toast

MAKES 2 SERVINGS
PREPARATION TIME - 10 MINUTES
COOKING TIME - 10 MINUTES
NUTRITIONAL VALUES PER SERVING - 287 KCALS, 21 G CARBS, 10 G PROTEIN, 9 G FAT

INGREDIENTS

- 4 slices bread, white or wholemeal
- 2 eggs
- 100 ml milk
- 1 tsp salt
- 1 tsp black pepper
- 50 g cheddar cheese, grated

METHOD

1. Preheat the air fryer to 180 degrees Celsius and line the bottom of the basket with parchment paper.
2. Cut the two slices of bread into 4 even rectangles.
3. In a mixing bowl, whisk the eggs until well beaten. Stir in a sprinkle of salt and black pepper
4. Soak the bread slices in the egg mixture for a few minutes until they are fully covered and have become soggy.
5. Transfer the eggy bread to the air fryer basket and shut the lid. Cook for 5-6 minutes until the bread has become crispy and slightly browned on the edges.
6. Open the lid of the air fryer and sprinkle the cheese evenly over the top of each slice. Shut the lid and continue cooking for another 5 minutes until the cheese has melted.
7. Serve with a sauce of your choice for breakfast.

Air Fryer Hash Browns

MAKES 4 SERVINGS
PREPARATION TIME - 5 MINUTES
COOKING TIME - 10 MINUTES
NUTRITIONAL VALUES PER SERVING - 112 KCALS, 13 G CARBS, 5 G PROTEIN, 6 G FAT

INGREDIENTS

- 4 white potatoes, peeled and shredded
- 1 onion, peeled and shredded
- 1 tbsp olive oil
- ½ tsp black pepper
- ½ tsp salt

METHOD

1. Place the potatoes in a bowl and stir in the onions, olive oil, black pepper, and salt. Shape into hash browns and transfer to the air fryer.
2. Cook on a high heat for 10 minutes, flipping halfway through, until hot, crispy, and browned on the edges.
3. Serve the hash browns as part of your breakfast while they're still piping hot.

Air Fryer Omelette

MAKES 2 SERVINGS
PREPARATION TIME - 5 MINUTES
COOKING TIME - 10 MINUTES
NUTRITIONAL VALUES PER SERVING - 176 KCALS, 11 G CARBS, 7 G PROTEIN, 12 G FAT

INGREDIENTS

- 4 eggs
- 100 ml milk
- ½ tsp black pepper
- ½ red pepper, deseeded and finely sliced
- 100 g cheddar cheese, grated

METHOD

1. In a small bowl, whisk together the eggs and milk until fully combined. Add a small amount of black pepper and stir in the red pepper slices.
2. Pour the egg mixture into a well-greased round pan and transfer to the air fryer. Shut the lid and turn the air fryer onto 200 degrees Celsius.
3. Cook the omelette for 10 minutes until it begins to set. Open the lid of the air fryer and sprinkle the cheddar cheese evenly over the top of the omelette and continue cooking for a further five minutes until the cheese has melted.
4. Use a spatula to transfer the omelette from the pan to a plate. Eat while the omelette is still hot with a garnish or sauce of your choice.

LUNCH

Your air fryer can also be used to create delicious lunch dishes too! On the days where you're at home and have extra time to create something a little more extravagant for your lunch, your air fryer should be a go-to! There is an endless variation in the types of lunch-appropriate recipes that you can follow using your air fryer.

Give the recipes below a go when you've got a day at home and want to make something more exciting than a sandwich!

Air Fryer Crispy Root Vegetables

MAKES 4 SERVINGS
PREPARATION TIME - 5 MINUTES
COOKING TIME - 15 MINUTES
NUTRITIONAL VALUES PER SERVING - 101 KCALS, 12 G CARBS, 4 G PROTEIN, 3 G FAT

INGREDIENTS

- 4 carrots, peeled and chopped into long chunks
- 4 parsnips, peeled and chopped into long chunks
- 1 swede, peeled and chopped into long chunks
- 2 tbsp olive oil
- 1 tbsp dried mixed herbs

METHOD

1. Preheat the air fryer to 150 degrees Celsius and line the bottom of the basket with parchment paper.
2. Place the chopped carrots, parsnips, and swede in a large bowl. Drizzle the olive oil over the vegetables and sprinkle the dried herbs into the bowl. Toss to coat.
3. Place the vegetables into the air fryer basket and shut the lid. Cook for 15 minutes until the vegetables are all well cooked and crispy.
4. Serve as part of your lunch while the vegetables are still hot.

Air Fryer Crispy Chips

MAKES 4 SERVINGS
PREPARATION TIME - 10 MINUTES
COOKING TIME - 30 MINUTES
NUTRITIONAL VALUE PER SERVING - 140 CALORIES, 21 CARBOHYDRATES, 4 FAT, 1 G PROTEIN

INGREDIENTS

- ◆ 4 white potatoes
- ◆ 1 tbsp olive oil

METHOD

1. Preheat the air fryer to a medium heat setting.
2. Peel the potatoes and slice them into batons. Place in a bowl and toss in olive oil to fully coat on all sides.
3. Transfer to the air fryer and shut the lid. Cook for 30 minutes until crispy and golden.
4. Serve the chips while stewing hot as a side to your main dish.

Air Fryer Crispy Pizza

MAKES 4 SERVINGS
PREPARATION TIME - 15 MINUTES
COOKING TIME - 10 MINUTES
NUTRITIONAL VALUES PER SERVING - 220 KCALS, 17 G CARBS, 7 G PROTEIN, 9 G FAT

INGREDIENTS

FOR THE PIZZA DOUGH:

- 400 g plain flour
- 1 tsp salt
- 1 tbsp dry non-fast-acting yeast
- 400 ml warm water

FOR THE TOPPINGS:

- 100 g tomato paste
- 100 g mozzarella cheese, grated
- Additional toppings of your choice

METHOD

1. To make the pizza dough, whisk together the plain flour, salt, and dry yeast in a large mixing bowl. Pour in the warm water in small batches and stir well to form a tacky dough.

2. Lightly dust a clean surface in your kitchen with plain flour and roll the dough out until it is around ½ an inch thick.

3. Preheat the air fryer to 150 degrees Celsius and line the bottom of the basket with parchment paper.

4. Spread the tomato paste along the surface of the dough in an even layer. Top with the grated mozzarella cheese and any additional toppings that you want on your pizza.

5. Add the pizza to the air fryer and cook the pizza for 10 minutes until the crust is golden and crispy, and the cheese is starting to bubble and turn brown.

6. Serve the pizza while it is still piping hot with a side salad.

Air Fryer White Fish Cakes

MAKES 2 SERVINGS
PREPARATION TIME - 10 MINUTES
COOKING TIME - 10 MINUTES
NUTRITIONAL VALUES PER SERVING - 219 KCALS, 12 G CARBS, 25 G PROTEIN, 5 G FAT

INGREDIENTS

- 400 g white fish
- 1 white onion, peeled and finely sliced
- 1 tsp dried chives
- 1 tsp black pepper
- 2 tbsp plain flour
- 2 eggs, beaten
- 100 g breadcrumbs
- 100 ml milk (any kind)

METHOD

1. Preheat the air fryer to 180 degrees Celsius. and line the air fryer mesh basket with greaseproof paper.
2. Chop the white fish and place in a large bowl. Add the white onion, dried chives, and black pepper, and stir well to combine.
3. Shape the mixture into circular patties.
4. Place the flour in one bowl, the beaten eggs in another, and the breadcrumbs in a third bowl. Dip the patties into the flour, then the eggs, and finally in the breadcrumbs to fully coat them.
5. Transfer the patties to the air fryer and cook for 8-10 minutes until hot and crispy. Serve with a side salad.

Air Fryer Chickpea Falafel

MAKES 4 SERVINGS
PREPARATION TIME - 10 MINUTES
COOKING TIME - 15 MINUTES
NUTRITIONAL VALUES PER SERVING - 158 KCALS, 13 G CARBS, 9 G PROTEIN, 8 G FAT

INGREDIENTS

- ◆ 1 white onion, peeled and sliced
- ◆ 4 cloves garlic, peeled and sliced
- ◆ 2 tbsp fresh parsley leaves, finely chopped
- ◆ 2 tbsp fresh coriander leaves, finely chopped
- ◆ 1 tsp chili powder
- ◆ ½ tsp ground cumin
- ◆ 2 x 400 g cans of chickpeas, drained and rinsed
- ◆ 1 tsp salt
- ◆ 1 tsp baking powder
- ◆ 1 tsp dried mixed herbs

METHOD

1. Line the bottom of the air fryer basket with parchment paper.

2. Place the white onion, garlic cloves, fresh parsley, and fresh coriander in a blender and pulse for 30-60 seconds until they form a smooth mixture. Transfer to a bowl.

3. Add the chickpeas to the blender and pulse until the chickpeas are like a smooth paste. Transfer to the same bowl as the onion, garlic, and fresh herbs.

4. Add the chili powder, ground cumin, salt, baking powder, and dried mixed herbs to the bowl and stir well. Add some water if the mixture looks too dry. It should have a paste-like texture.

5. Scoop 2 tbsp of the mixture at a time and roll into small balls. Place the falafel balls into the prepared air fryer basket, shut the lid, and turn the machine onto a heat setting of around 200 degrees Celsius. Cook the falafel for 15 minutes until golden and crispy.

6. Serve the falafels hot or cold either in a wrap, on a salad, or on their own. Store leftovers in the fridge for no more than 3 days.

Air Fryer Tempeh Noodle Soup

MAKES 4 SERVINGS
PREPARATION TIME - 15 MINUTES
COOKING TIME - 15 MINUTES
NUTRITIONAL VALUE PER SERVING - 376 KCALS, 28 G CARBS, 32 G PROTEIN, 15 G FAT

INGREDIENTS

- 2 x vegetable stock cubes
- 1 x 400 g block of tempeh, diced
- 1 white onion, peeled and finely sliced
- 1 clove garlic, peeled and crushed
- 2 carrots, peeled and finely sliced
- 1 leek, finely chopped
- 50 g mange tout
- 1 tsp salt
- 1 tsp black pepper
- 4 nests of dry white or wholemeal noodles

1. Cover the inner basket of the air fryer with olive oil or greaseproof paper.
2. Dissolve the vegetable stock cubes in the required amount of boiling water as per the packet and pour into the prepared air fryer basket.
3. In a large bowl, add the diced tempeh, white onion, garlic clove, carrots, leek, mange tout, salt, and black pepper. Combine well and transfer to the air fryer.
4. Close the lid and switch the air fryer to 200 degrees Celsius. Cook for 15 minutes until the ingredients are well-cooked.
5. While the air fryer is on, boil a pan of water and add the noodles. Lower the heat to a gentle simmer and cook for 10 minutes until the noodles are soft and well-cooked.
6. Serve the noodles evenly into four bowls and serve with the hot, crispy tempeh on top.

Air Fryer Salmon

MAKES 4 SERVINGS
PREPARATION TIME - 10 MINUTES
COOKING TIME - 10 MINUTES
NUTRITIONAL VALUES PER SERVING - 145 KCALS, 3 G CARBS, 21 G PROTEIN, 10 G FAT

INGREDIENTS

- 4 x 150 g fillets salmon
- 1 tsp olive oil
- ½ tsp black pepper
- Juice of 1 lemon

METHOD

1. Rinse the salmon fillets and pat dry with paper towels.
2. Coat the fillets on both sides with olive oil and top one side with black pepper, and the juice of 1 lemon.
3. Transfer the salmon fillets to the air fryer basket, seasoned side facing up. Turn the air fryer to a heat of around 180 degrees Celsius. Close the lid and cook the salmon fillets for 10 minutes, turning halfway through, until flaky.
4. Serve the salmon fillets hot with a sauce of your choice.

Air Fryer Fish

MAKES 4 SERVINGS
PREPARATION TIME - 15 MINUTES
COOKING TIME - 15 MINUTES
NUTRITIONAL VALUE PER SERVING - 187 KCALS, 8 G CARBS, 23 G PROTEIN, 4 G FAT

INGREDIENTS

- 8 x 100 g fresh fish fillets
- 1 tbsp olive oil
- 50 g dry breadcrumbs
- ½ tsp paprika
- ½ tsp chili powder
- ½ tsp salt
- ½ tsp ground black pepper
- 1 tsp tartar sauce
- Zest 1 lemon

METHOD

1. Preheat the air fryer to 200 degrees Celsius. Brush the fish fillets lightly with olive oil.
2. In a bowl, mix the breadcrumbs, paprika, chili powder, salt, black pepper, and garlic powder.
3. Roll the fish fillets in the bread crumb mixture until fully coated. Transfer to the air fryer basket.
4. Cook the fish for 12-15 minutes, turning halfway through, until well cooked and flaky.

Air Fryer Fresh Tomato and Parsnip Soup

MAKES 8 SERVINGS
PREPARATION TIME - 15 MINUTES
COOKING TIME - 15 MINUTES
NUTRITIONAL VALUE PER SERVING - 147 KCALS, 16 G CARBS, 4 G PROTEIN, 6 G FAT

INGREDIENTS

- 1 tbsp olive oil
- 1 white onion, peeled and chopped
- 1 clove garlic, peeled and crushed
- 1 parsnip, peeled and finely sliced
- 200 g fresh beef tomatoes, quartered
- 1 x 400 g can of chopped tomatoes
- 1 tsp brown sugar
- 1 tsp black pepper
- 1 tsp dried oregano

METHOD

1. Heat 1 tbsp olive oil in a frying pan.
2. Add the onions and garlic and cook over medium heat for 8-10 minutes until they begin to soften and become aromatic.
3. Transfer the onions and garlic to the air fryer and add the parsnips, beef tomatoes, chopped tomatoes, brown sugar, black pepper, and dried oregano. Stir well.
4. Shut the lid of the air fryer and turn to a heat of 200 degrees Celsius. Cook for 15 minutes until the soup is hot.
5. Transfer the hot soup to a blender or food processor. Pulse the soup in 30-second intervals until smooth and consistent.
6. Serve the soup while steaming hot with a side of crusty bread and butter.

Air Fryer Hot and Cheesy Broccoli

MAKES 8 SERVINGS
PREPARATION TIME - 10 MINUTES
COOKING TIME - 15 MINUTES
NUTRITIONAL VALUES PER SERVING - 113 KCALS, 7 G CARBS, 3 G PROTEIN, 5 G FAT

INGREDIENTS

- 1 broccoli, broken into florets
- 4 tbsp hot sauce
- 2 tbsp olive oil
- 1 tsp garlic powder
- ½ tsp salt
- ½ tsp black pepper
- 1 tbsp plain flour
- 1 tbsp corn starch
- 50 g cheddar cheese, grated

METHOD

1. Preheat the air fryer to 180 degrees Celsius and line the bottom of the basket with parchment paper.
2. In a bowl, combine the hot sauce, olive oil, garlic powder, salt, and black pepper. Add the broccoli to the bowl and toss to coat in the sauce.
3. Stir the plain flour and corn starch into the bowl and mix well.
4. Transfer the broccoli to the lined basket in the air fryer, close the lid, and cook for 12 minutes until the broccoli has softened and is golden in colour.
5. Open the lid of the air fryer and sprinkle the cheese over the top of the cauliflower. Shut the lid and cook for a further 3-5 minutes until the cheese has melted.
6. Serve the broccoli as a side to your dinner.

Air Fryer Tofu

MAKES 4 SERVINGS
PREPARATION TIME - 10 MINUTES
COOKING TIME - 15 MINUTES
NUTRITIONAL VALUE PER SERVING - 299 KCALS, 25 G CARBS, 28 G PROTEIN, 17 G FAT

INGREDIENTS

- 1 x 400 g block of firm tofu, diced
- 2 tbsp soy sauce
- 1 tbsp honey
- 1 tbsp white vinegar
- 1 white onion, peeled and finely sliced
- 2 x vegetable stock cubes
- 2 carrots, peeled and chopped
- 50 g baby sweetcorn
- 50 g carrots, sliced
- 50 g mange tout
- 1 tsp black pepper

METHOD

1. Coat the inner compartment of the air fryer with olive oil or cover it with greaseproof paper.
2. Place the diced tofu in a bowl. In a separate small mixing bowl, combine the soy sauce, honey, and white vinegar.
3. Toss the tofu in the sauce until fully coated and set aside.
4. Dissolve the vegetable stock cubes in boiling water following the packet instructions. Pour this into the prepared air fryer basket.
5. Add the coated tofu, onion, carrots, baby sweetcorn, carrots, mange tout, and black pepper to the air fryer.
6. Close the lid of the air fryer and cook for 15 minutes at 200 degrees Celsius.
7. Serve the tofu while hot with a carbohydrate of your choice and some freshly-cooked vegetables.

Air Fryer Hot Chicken Wings

MAKES 4 SERVINGS
PREPARATION TIME - 5 MINUTES
COOKING TIME - 10 MINUTES
NUTRITIONAL VALUE PER SERVING - 318 KCALS, 16 G CARBS, 24 G PROTEIN, 13 G FAT

INGREDIENTS

- ◆ 3 tsp hot sauce
- ◆ 2 tbsp soy sauce
- ◆ 3 tbsp honey
- ◆ Zest 1 lemon
- ◆ 4 x 100 g chicken wings
- ◆ 4 tbsp corn starch
- ◆ 1 tbsp sesame seeds
- ◆ 1 tbsp dried chives
- ◆ 1 tsp black pepper

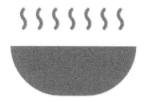

METHOD

1. Coat the basket of the air fryer with olive oil or cover it with greaseproof paper.
2. In a bowl, whisk together the hot sauce, soy sauce, honey, and lemon zest.
3. Take each of the chicken wings one at a time, and gently roll in the sauce to coat on all sides.
4. Transfer the chicken wings to the prepared tray of the air fryer, making sure they aren't touching each other, and close the lid.
5. Cook the wings on a heat setting of 200 degrees Celsius for 10 minutes until they are fully cooked and crispy.
6. In a bowl, mix 4 tbsp corn starch with 1 tbsp water and stir well to form a smooth mixture. Stir in the sesame seeds, dried chives, and black pepper.
7. Remove the chicken wings from the air fryer and coat in the cornstarch mixture. Place back into the air fryer and cook for a further 5 minutes.
8. Serve the chicken wings with a side of your choice and an extra drizzle of hot sauce.

Air Fryer Pulled BBQ Jackfruit

MAKES 4 SERVINGS
PREPARATION TIME - 10 MINUTES
COOKING TIME - 10 MINUTES
NUTRITIONAL VALUE PER SERVING - 214 KCALS, 16 G CARBS, 8 G PROTEIN, 7 G FAT

INGREDIENTS

- 1 onion, finely sliced
- 4 tbsp BBQ sauce
- 2 tbsp BBQ seasoning
- 1 tsp smoked paprika
- 1 tsp garlic powder
- 1 tsp black pepper
- 400 g jackfruit

METHOD

1. Coat the basket of the air fryer with olive oil or cover it with greaseproof paper.
2. In a bowl, mix together the BBQ sauce, BBQ seasoning, smoked paprika, garlic powder, and black pepper.
3. Use a fork to pull the jackfruit into stringy pieces. Add the jackfruit to the bowl and toss to coat.
4. Transfer the jackfruit to the lined air fryer basket and close the lid. Turn the air fryer onto a low heat setting and cook the BBQ jackfruit for 10 minutes.
5. Serve the BBQ jackfruit inside a burger bun with a side of chips and salad.

Air Fryer Spaghetti and Meatballs

MAKES 4 SERVINGS
PREPARATION TIME - 15 MINUTES
COOKING TIME - 15 MINUTES
NUTRITIONAL VALUE PER SERVING - 256 KCALS, 20 G CARBS, 15 G PROTEIN, 17 G FAT

INGREDIENTS

- 1 x 400 g jar of tomato and vegetable pasta sauce
- 400 g ground beef
- 2 eggs, beaten
- 1 tbsp soy sauce
- 200 g breadcrumbs
- 1 tsp black pepper
- 1 tsp dried chives
- 4 x 100 g nests spaghetti, dry and uncooked
- 1 tsp salt
- 100 g cheddar cheese, grated

METHOD

1. Use greaseproof paper to line the air fryer basket.
2. Pour the marinara sauce into the lined air fryer basket.
3. Place the ground beef in a large bowl and whisk in the eggs and soy sauce.
4. Stir the breadcrumbs, black pepper, and dried chives into the bowl and mix well.
5. Using a spoon or your hands, create small balls of even size until you have used all of the meat mixture.
6. Place the balls into the marinara sauce that is already in the air fryer.
7. Close the lid and cook the meatballs at 200 degrees Celsius for 25 minutes until the meat is fully cooked and the edges have started to turn crispy.
8. While the meatballs are in the air fryer, boil a large pan of water. Add the spaghetti and a sprinkle of salt. Cook for 10-12 minutes until the spaghetti has slightly softened.
9. Split the spaghetti evenly in four bowls and top with the meatball and marinara mixture.
10. Top each bowl with a sprinkle of grated cheese and enjoy!

Air Fryer Chicken Nuggets

MAKES 8 SERVINGS
PREPARATION TIME - 15 MINUTES
COOKING TIME - 15 MINUTES
NUTRITIONAL VALUES PER SERVING - 265 KCALS, 11 G CARBS, 15 G PROTEIN, 8 G FAT

INGREDIENTS

- 4 x 100 g skinless, boneless chicken breast fillets
- 2 eggs, beaten
- 1 tbsp smoked paprika
- 1 tsp Cajun pepper
- 1 tsp garlic powder
- 1 tsp black pepper
- 100 g breadcrumbs

METHOD

1. Preheat the air fryer to 200 degrees Celsius and line the bottom of the basket with parchment paper.
2. Cut the chicken breasts into small, even chunks and set aside.
3. Beat the eggs into a bowl and add the smoked paprika, Cajun pepper, garlic powder, and black pepper. Whisk to mix well.
4. Place the breadcrumbs in a bowl.
5. Cover the chicken breast chunks with the beaten egg and spice mixture.
6. Roll the chicken breasts in the breadcrumbs to fully coat each fillet.
7. Transfer the covered chicken breast chunks into the lined air fryer basket. Shut the lid and cook for 12-15 minutes until crispy and golden.
8. Serve with a side and sauce of your choice.

Air Fryer Tofu with Honey Garlic Sauce

MAKES 8 SERVINGS
PREPARATION TIME - 15 MINUTES
COOKING TIME - 15 MINUTES
NUTRITIONAL VALUES PER SERVING - 278 KCALS, 12 G CARBS, 18 G PROTEIN, 12 G FAT

INGREDIENTS

FOR THE TOFU:

- 1 x 400 g block extra firm tofu
- 1 tbsp corn starch
- 1 tsp garlic powder
- 1 tsp paprika
- ½ tsp Salt
- ½ tsp black pepper

FOR THE HONEY GARLIC SAUCE:

- 4 tbsp honey
- 2 tbsp soy sauce
- 2 tsp garlic, minced
- ½ tsp ground ginger
- ½ tbsp corn starch

METHOD

1. Preheat the air fryer to 200 degrees Celsius and line the bottom of the basket with parchment paper.
2. Place the tofu on clean paper towels to drain out any excess moisture. Cut the tofu into small, even chunks.
3. Place the tofu in a bowl. In a separate bowl, combine the corn starch, paprika, garlic powder, salt, and black pepper.
4. Add the corn starch and spice mixture to the bowl of tofu. Toss to fully coat the tofu and cover the bowl with a clean towel or some clingfilm. Leave to marinate for 10 minutes.
5. Transfer the tofu to the air fryer basket and shut the lid. Cook for 15 minutes until the tofu is slightly browned and crispy.
6. While the tofu is cooking, create the honey garlic sauce by combining all of the ingredients in a bowl. Whisk well and place in a small saucepan over a high heat. Warm for a few minutes, stirring frequently, until the sauce it hot.
7. After the tofu has been cooking for 15 minutes, remove it from the air fryer and coat in half of the honey garlic sauce. Return to the air fryer and cook for a few extra minutes.
8. Serve the tofu with the remaining honey garlic sauce drizzled over the top.

Air Fryer Spicy Bean Burgers

MAKES 4 SERVINGS
PREPARATION TIME - 15 MINUTES
COOKING TIME - 15 MINUTES
NUTRITIONAL VALUES PER SERVING - 276 KCALS, 24 G CARBS, 16 G PROTEIN, 10 G FAT

INGREDIENTS

- 1 x 400 g can black beans
- 100 g panko breadcrumbs
- 1 beef tomato, sliced
- 1 jalapeno pepper, finely chopped
- 1 egg, beaten

- 1 tsp fresh herb of your choice, finely chopped
- 1 clove garlic, minced
- 1 tsp Cajun pepper
- 1 tsp paprika
- 1 tsp black pepper
- 4 burger buns, split into halves

METHOD

1. Preheat the air fryer to 200 degrees Celsius. Rinse and drain the black beans, and place them in a bowl.
2. Place the beans into a blender, pulses until smooth, and transfer to a bowl. Add the rest of the ingredients, aside from the burger buns.
3. Once blended, transfer to a large bowl.
4. Stir in the breadcrumbs, beef tomato, jalapeno pepper, egg, fresh herbs, garlic, Cajun pepper, paprika, and black pepper. Mix until well combined.
5. Shape the bean mixture into four even patties and transfer to the air fryer. Close the lid and cook for 10-15 minutes until hot and crispy.
6. Serve the burgers while still hot inside the burger buns with some salad and sauce.

Air Fryer Ratatouille

MAKES 2 SERVINGS
PREPARATION TIME - 10 MINUTES
COOKING TIME - 10 MINUTES
NUTRITIONAL VALUE PER SERVING - 155 CALORIES, 18 G
CARBOHYDRATES, 9 G FAT, 14 G PROTEIN

INGREDIENTS

- 4 beef tomatoes, sliced
- 2 cloves garlic, minced
- 1 courgette, cut into chunks
- 1 red pepper, deseeded and cut into chunks
- 1 yellow pepper, deseeded and cut into chunks
- 1 tbsp olive oil

- 4 tbsp tomato paste
- 1 x 400 g can chopped tomatoes
- 2 tbsp mixed herbs
- ½ tsp salt
- ½ tsp black pepper
- 1 tsp dried chives

METHOD

1. Preheat the air fryer to 180 degrees Celsius and line the air fryer with parchment paper.
2. In a large bowl, add the olive oil, add the beef tomatoes, garlic cloves, courgette, red pepper, and yellow pepper.
3. Stir in the olive oil, tomato paste, and chopped tomatoes. Sprinkle the herbs, salt, and pepper into the bowl and stir well.
4. Transfer the ratatouille to the air fryer basket and shut the lid. Heat for 10-12 minutes until the vegetables have softened and the ratatouille is hot.
5. Serve the ratatouille hot with a side of crusty bread.

Air Fryer Tuna and Sweetcorn Jacket Potato

MAKES 1 SERVING
PREPARATION TIME - 10 MINUTES
COOKING TIME - 15 MINUTES
NUTRITIONAL VALUES PER SERVING - 324 KCALS, 28 G CARBS, 17 G PROTEIN, 13 G FAT

INGREDIENTS

- 1 x 200 g canned tuna, drained
- 2 tbsp mayonnaise
- 50 g sweetcorn
- ½ tsp black pepper
- 1 large jacket potato
- 100 g cheddar cheese, grated

METHOD

1. Preheat the air fryer to 200 degrees Celsius and line the air fryer basket with parchment paper.
2. In a mixing bowl, add the tuna, mayonnaise, sweetcorn, and black pepper. Stir together until a smooth mixture is formed.
3. Cut the top of jacket potato using a sharp knife and spoon the tuna filling inside.
4. Transfer the jacket potato to the air fryer and shut the lid. Cook for 10 minutes until the jacket potato is browned and crispy.
5. Open the air fryer lid and sprinkle the cheddar cheese on top of the jacket potato. Shut the lid once again and continue cooking for a little longer until the cheese has softened.
6. Serve the jacket potato while still piping hot with a side of your choice.

Air Fryer Veggie Croquettes

MAKES 4 SERVINGS
PREPARATION TIME - 15 MINUTES
COOKING TIME - 15 MINUTES
NUTRITIONAL VALUES PER SERVING - 214 KCALS, 19 G CARBS, 6 G PROTEIN, 8 G FAT

INGREDIENTS

- ◆ 200 g white potato, peeled
- ◆ 50 g fresh or canned peas
- ◆ 1 onion, finely sliced
- ◆ 2 cloves garlic, finely sliced
- ◆ 50 g parmesan cheese, grated
- ◆ 1 tsp salt
- ◆ 1 tsp black pepper
- ◆ 1 tsp dried chives
- ◆ 2 eggs, beaten
- ◆ 100 g breadcrumbs

METHOD

1. Add the peeled white potatoes to a saucepan of boiling water. Cook for 10-12 minutes until the potatoes are soft.
2. Transfer the potatoes to a large mixing bowl and use a potato masher to mash them until there are no lumps.
3. Add the peas, onion, garlic, beaten eggs, parmesan cheese, salt, black pepper, and dried chives to the bowl. Mix well.
4. Whisk one egg into the mixture and stir until combined.
5. Place the other egg in a separate bowl and whisk well. Place the breadcrumbs into a third bowl.
6. Shape the potato mixture into 12 even-sized croquettes.
7. Lightly brush the croquettes with the beaten egg mixture and then roll in the breadcrumbs to fully cover them.
8. Transfer the croquettes to the air fryer and turn the heat onto 180 degrees Celsius. Cook for 10-12 minutes until golden and crispy.
9. Serve the croquettes as a side for lunch.

Healthy Air Fryer Beetroot Burgers

MAKES 4 SERVINGS
PREPARATION TIME - 15 MINUTES
COOKING TIME - 15 MINUTES
NUTRITIONAL VALUES PER SERVING - 342 KCALS, 23 G CARBS, 15 G PROTEIN, 14 G FAT

INGREDIENTS

- 1 white potato, peeled
- 4 beets, peeled and finely chopped
- 1 tsp cayenne pepper
- 1 tsp cumin powder
- 1 tsp garlic powder
- 1 tsp onion powder
- 1 tsp dried thyme
- 4 tbsp nutritional yeast
- 50 g breadcrumbs
- 4 burger buns

1. Place the potatoes in a saucepan of boiling water and cook for 12 minutes until soft. Remove from the pan and mash until there are just a few small lumps. Place the potatoes into a bowl.

2. Place the beets into a food processor and pulse until smooth.

3. Add the cayenne pepper, cumin powder, garlic powder, onion powder, dried thyme, and nutritional yeast into the bowl with the potatoes. Stir well and fold in the beets.

4. Stir in the breadcrumbs and create four even patties with the mixture.

5. Transfer the patties to the air fryer, shut the lid, and turn the machine onto 180 degrees Celsius.

6. Cook the burgers for 10-12 minutes until hot and crispy.

7. Serve the burgers in buns with salad and sauce, with a side of chips or vegetables.

DINNER

If you're searching for some new and exciting dishes to cook for dinner, your air fryer will come to the rescue! For a lot of people, dinner time is the perfect opportunity to follow exciting recipes that you don't have the chance to try during the day when you're busy.

Because air fryers are so versatile, there is an endless number of dinner recipes available, and you could literally create something different every night of the year if you wanted to! Below, we've got a wide range of delicious meat-based and meat-free dishes that you can cook for dinner using your air fryer.

Air Fryer Chicken New Yorker

MAKES 4 SERVINGS
PREPARATION TIME - 15 MINUTES
COOKING TIME - 15 MINUTES
NUTRITIONAL VALUES PER SERVING - 324 KCALS, 19 G CARBS, 26 G PROTEIN, 15 G FAT

INGREDIENTS

- ♦ 4 x 100 g skinless, boneless chicken breast fillets
- ♦ 50 g cheddar cheese, grated
- ♦ 1 tsp garlic powder
- ♦ 1 tsp dried mixed herbs
- ♦ 8 strips bacon, whole
- ♦ 4 tbsp smoky BBQ sauce
- ♦ 1 tsp salt
- ♦ 1 tsp black pepper

METHOD

1. Preheat the air fryer to 200 degrees Celsius and line the bottom of the basket with parchment paper.
2. Place the chicken breast fillets onto a clean surface.
3. In a mixing bowl, mix together the cheddar cheese, garlic powder, and dried mixed herbs until well combined.
4. Spoon the cheese onto the top of each chicken breast fillet.
5. Wrap each chicken breast fillet with two slices of bacon to seal in the cheese. Transfer to the lined air fryer basket and season with salt and pepper.
6. Close the lid of the air fryer and cook the chicken fillets for 10 minutes until the chicken is crispy and golden, and the cheese is hot and gooey. Open the air fryer lid and add 1 tbsp of BBQ sauce on top of each fillet. Shut the lid of the air fryer and continue cooking for a few extra minutes until the sauce is hot and sticky.
7. Serve the chicken New Yorker while still hot with a side of your choice.

Air Fryer Sticky Pork Ribs

MAKES 2 SERVINGS
PREPARATION TIME - 1 HOUR 10 MINUTES
COOKING TIME - 15 MINUTES
NUTRITIONAL VALUES PER SERVING - 301 KCALS, 9 G CARBS, 28 G PROTEIN, 23 G FAT

INGREDIENTS

- 400 g pork ribs
- 2 cloves garlic, minced
- 2 tbsp soy sauce
- 2 tbsp honey
- 1 tsp cayenne pepper
- 1 tsp chili flakes
- 1 tbsp olive oil
- 2 tbsp BBQ sauce
- 2 tbsp hot sauce
- 1 tsp salt
- 1 tsp black pepper

METHOD

1. Place the pork ribs on a clean surface.
2. In a mixing bowl, combine the minced garlic, soy sauce, honey, cayenne pepper, chili flakes, olive oil, BBQ sauce, hot sauce, salt, and black pepper.
3. Coat the pork ribs in the sauce and spice mixture until fully coated on all sides.
4. Leave the pork ribs to marinate in the bowl and cover with a clean tea towel or clingfilm.
5. Line the bottom of the basket with parchment paper. When the pork has been in the bowl for a full hour, transfer the ribs to the air fryer basket.
6. Shut the lid and cook for 15 minutes, turning them halfway through.
7. Once cooked, remove the ribs from the air fryer and serve with a side of your choice.

Air Fryer Vegetarian Soy 'Beef' Meatballs

MAKES 8 SERVINGS
PREPARATION TIME - 15 MINUTES
COOKING TIME - 1 HOUR 30 MINUTES
NUTRITIONAL VALUE PER SERVING - 355 CALORIES, 21 G
CARBOHYDRATES, 20 G FAT, 29 G PROTEIN

INGREDIENTS

- 200 g plain flour
- 100 g wholemeal crackers
- 2 eggs, beaten (or 4 tbsp apple sauce if you need a vegan alternative)
- 400 ml milk (any kind)
- 1 tsp onion powder
- 1 tsp garlic powder
- 1 tsp cayenne pepper
- 1 tsp Cajun pepper
- 1 tsp salt
- 1 tsp black pepper
- 800 g ground soy beef alternative

1. Preheat the air fryer to 180 degrees Celsius and line the bottom of the basket with parchment paper.

2. In a large bowl, whisk together the plain flour and wholemeal crackers.

3. Whisk in the beaten eggs or apple sauce and pour in the milk. Stir well to fully combine the ingredients.

4. Sprinkle in the onion powder, garlic powder, cayenne pepper, Cajun pepper, salt, and black pepper.

5. Fold the soy beef alternative into the bowl and stir to create a consistent mixture.

6. Spoon the beef or soy beef into small, even balls and transfer to the air fryer. Close the lid and cook for 12-15 minutes until crispy and browned.

7. Serve the meatballs while they're still hot with a side of pasta or spaghetti and a sauce of your choice.

Air Fryer Sweet Potato Burgers

MAKES 4 SERVINGS
PREPARATION TIME - 15 MINUTES
COOKING TIME - 30 MINUTES
NUTRITIONAL VALUE PER SERVING - 356 CALORIES, 41 G
CARBOHYDRATES, 21 G FAT, 29 G PROTEIN

INGREDIENTS

- 1 x 400 g can mixed beans
- 400 g sweet potato
- 1 small red onion, peeled and chopped
- 1 clove garlic
- 1 tbsp olive oil
- 1 tsp chili flakes
- 1 tsp smoked paprika
- ½ tsp black pepper
- ½ tsp salt
- 4 burger buns

METHOD

1. Preheat the air fryer to 200 degrees Celsius and line the bottom of the basket with parchment paper.
2. Drain and rinse the mixed beans. Place in a bowl and set aside.
3. Peel the sweet potato and cut into chunks. Heat a saucepan of water and cook the potatoes for 12-15 minutes until softened. Use a potato masher to mash the potatoes until there are no lumps.
4. Peel the onion and garlic clove and slice finely.
5. Heat 1 tbsp olive oil in a frying pan and add the garlic onion. Cook for 5-7 minutes until softened and fragrant.
6. Add the onions and garlic to the bowl with the sweet potato, along with the chili flakes, smoked paprika, black pepper, and salt.
7. Use a fork to mash the beans and add to the bowl with the other ingredients.
8. Shape the mixture into four even patties, about 1.5-2 inches thick. Transfer to the air fryer basket and shut the lid.
9. Cook the patties for 10-12 minutes until hot and crispy.
10. Serve each bean burger in a burger bun with salad and a sauce of your choice.

Crispy Air Fryer Tomato Roast Lamb

MAKES 8 SERVINGS
PREPARATION TIME - 15 MINUTES
COOKING TIME - 1 HOUR 30 MINUTES
NUTRITIONAL VALUE PER SERVING - 555 CALORIES, 33 G
CARBOHYDRATES, 32 G FAT, 41 G PROTEIN

INGREDIENTS

- 1 large leg of lamb, weighing around 3 kg
- 6 cloves of garlic, peeled and crushed
- 1 tbsp oregano
- Zest and juice of 1 lemon
- 6 tbsp olive oil
- 1 tsp salt
- 1 tsp black pepper
- 1 kg of new potatoes
- 1 x 400 g can of chopped tomatoes

METHOD

1. Preheat the air fryer to around 200 degrees Celsius.
2. Mix the crushed garlic, oregano, lemon zest and juice, olive oil, salt, and black pepper in a bowl until it forms a paste.
3. Poke small holes into the lamb and push the paste into the centre.
4. Transfer the lamb to the air fryer and add the new potatoes. Cook the lamb and potatoes in the air fryer for an hour.
5. Open the lid of the air fryer and stir in the chopped tomatoes. Shut the lid once again and cook for a further 30 minutes until the tomatoes are hot.
6. Serve the lamb for dinner while hot.

Air Fryer Chicken and Veggie Casserole

MAKES 4 SERVINGS
PREPARATION TIME - 15 MINUTES
COOKING TIME - 30 MINUTES
NUTRITIONAL VALUE PER SERVING - 368 KCALS, 34 G CARBS, 31 G PROTEIN, 18 G FAT

INGREDIENTS

- 1 tbsp olive oil
- 400 g chicken breast slices, diced
- 1 white onion, finely sliced
- ½ red pepper, finely sliced
- ½ yellow pepper, finely sliced
- 1 carrot, finely sliced
- 1 stick celery, finely sliced
- 4 eggs, beaten
- 200 ml milk (any type)
- 2 tbsp plain flour
- 1 tsp salt
- 50 g cheddar cheese, grated
- 1 tsp black pepper

METHOD

1. Heat the olive oil in a large frying pan and add the chicken breast slices. Cook for 10 minutes until browned. Transfer to the air fryer.
2. Add the white onion, red pepper, yellow pepper, carrot, and celery to the air fryer.
3. In a bowl, whisk together the eggs, milk, flour, and salt. Pour this mixture into air fryer, fully covering the chicken and vegetables.
4. Turn the air fryer onto a heat of around 200 degrees and close the lid. Cook the casserole for 20 minutes until hot.
5. Open the lid of the air fryer and sprinkle in the cheese and black pepper. Close the lid again and cook for a further 10 minutes until the cheddar cheese has melted.
6. Serve the casserole with some dumplings or noodles for lunch.

Air Fryer Egg, Cheese, and Ham Casserole

MAKES 4 SERVINGS
PREPARATION TIME - 10 MINUTES
COOKING TIME - 10 MINUTES
NUTRITIONAL VALUE PER SERVING - 455 KCALS, 19 G CARBS, 32 G PROTEIN, 33 G FAT

INGREDIENTS

- 8 eggs, beaten
- 200 ml milk
- 1 tsp salt
- 1 tsp black pepper
- 200 g smoked ham, pre-cooked and chopped
- 50 g cheddar cheese, grated

METHOD

1. In a large mixing bowl, whisk together the eggs, milk, salt, and black pepper until well combined.
2. Stir in half of the precooked smoked ham and transfer the mixture into the air fryer. Sprinkle the remaining ham and cheddar cheese over the top.
3. Close the lid of the air fryer and cook on a heat of 240 degrees Celsius for 10 minutes.
4. Serve the casserole while hot for dinner.

Air Fryer Beef and Mushrooms

MAKES 4 SERVINGS
PREPARATION TIME - 5 MINUTES
COOKING TIME - 15 MINUTES
NUTRITIONAL VALUES PER SERVING - 358 KCALS, 24 G CARBS, 33 G PROTEIN, 15 G FAT

INGREDIENTS

- 4 x beef stock cubes
- 4 tbsp olive oil
- 1 white onion, peeled and chopped
- 200 g sour cream
- 200 g mushroom, finely sliced
- 500 g steak, chopped

METHOD

1. Preheat the air fryer to 200 degrees Celsius and line the bottom of the basket with parchment paper or grease it with olive oil.
2. Dissolve the 4 beef stock cubes in boiling water and pour into the air fryer basket, being careful not to splash any.
3. Stir together the olive oil, white onion, sour cream, mushrooms, and steak chunks. Add to the air fryer and shut the lid of the machine.
4. Cook for 15 minutes until the steak is fully cooked all the way through. Serve the beef while it's still hot with a side of potatoes or rice and veggies.

Tomato and Cheese Chicken

MAKES 4 SERVINGS
PREPARATION TIME - 10 MINUTES
COOKING TIME - 15 MINUTES
NUTRITIONAL VALUES PER SERVING - 276 KCALS, 14 G CARBS, 27 G PROTEIN, 9 G FAT

INGREDIENTS

- 4 x 100 g chicken breast fillets
- 1 tbsp tomato paste
- 1 x 400 g can chopped tomatoes
- 1 tsp dried mixed herbs
- 50 g cheddar cheese, grated

METHOD

1. Preheat the air fryer to 180 degrees Celsius and line the bottom of the basket with parchment paper.
2. Cover the chicken breast fillets with tomato paste and add the dried mixed herbs on top.
3. Transfer the chicken breast fillets to the air fryer basket and pour the chopped tomatoes over the top. Close the lid of the air fryer and cook the chicken for 1- minutes, turning halfway through. They should be golden and crispy.
4. Open the air fryer lid and add the grated cheddar cheese on top of each of the chicken breasts. Shut the lid and continue cooking until the cheese has softened.
5. Serve the chicken breasts while still hot with sides of your choice.

Air Fryer Southern Fried Chicken

MAKES 4 SERVINGS
PREPARATION TIME - 10 MINUTES
COOKING TIME - 15 MINUTES
NUTRITIONAL VALUES PER SERVING - 298 KCALS, 17 G CARBS, 26 G PROTEIN, 12 G FAT

INGREDIENTS

- 200 g breadcrumbs
- 1 tsp dried basil
- 1 tsp smoked paprika
- 1 tsp BBQ seasoning
- 1 tsp chili flakes

- 1 tsp black pepper
- 1 tsp salt
- 1 egg
- 4 x 150 g chicken breast fillets, skinless and boneless

METHOD

1. Place the breadcrumbs in a mixing bowl and stir in the dried basil, smoked paprika, BBQ seasoning, chili flakes, black pepper, and salt.
2. In a separate bowl, whisk the egg until well beaten. Dip the chicken breast fillets into the egg mixture and roll the into the breadcrumbs to fully coat.
3. Transfer the chicken breast fillets to the lined air fryer basket and turn the heat to 200 degrees Celsius. Cook for 15 minutes until hot, golden, and crispy.

Air Fryer BBQ Beans and Lentils

MAKES 4 SERVINGS
PREPARATION TIME - 10 MINUTES
COOKING TIME - 10 MINUTES
NUTRITIONAL VALUE PER SERVING - 200 KCALS, 31 G CARBS, 21 G PROTEIN, 6 G FAT

INGREDIENTS

- 200 g dry red lentils
- 1 x 400 g can kidney beans
- 1 clove garlic, peeled and crushed
- 1 tbsp chili powder
- 1 tbsp BBQ seasoning
- 4 tbsp BBQ sauce
- 1 x 400 g can of chopped tomatoes
- 400 ml water

METHOD

1. In a large mixing bowl, add the dry red lentils. Drain and rinse the kidney beans, and add to the bowl.
2. Stir in the garlic, chili powder, BBQ seasoning, and BBQ sauce, and stir well until fully combined.
3. Transfer to the air fryer and pour in the chopped tomatoes and water.
4. Close the lid of the air fryer and cook at 200 degrees Celsius for 10 minutes until the lentils have fully absorbed the water and are soft.
5. Serve while hot with any extras of your choice.

Air Fryer Tofu Satay

MAKES 4 SERVINGS
PREPARATION TIME - 30 MINUTES
COOKING TIME - 10 MINUTES
NUTRITIONAL VALUES PER SERVING - 212 KCALS, 7 G CARBS, 23 G PROTEIN, 15 G FAT

INGREDIENTS

- 1 x 400 g block of firm tofu
- 3 tbsp soy sauce
- 2 tbsp hot sauce
- 1 tsp vinegar
- 1 tbsp peanut butter
- 2 tbsp brown sugar
- 2 tsp garlic powder
- 2 tsp ground ginger
- 2 tsp ground cumin
- 50 g roasted peanuts, chopped

METHOD

1. Remove the tofu from the packet and cut it into even-sized cubes.
2. Place the tofu into a large bowl. In a separate bowl, whisk together the soy sauce, hot sauce, vinegar, peanut butter, brown sugar, garlic powder, ground ginger, and ground cumin until well combined.
3. Toss the tofu in the sauce mixture until fully coated on all sides. Cover the bowl with a clean tea towel and set aside for 30 minutes to marinate.
4. Preheat the air fryer to 200 degrees Celsius and line the bottom of the basket with parchment paper.
5. Place the tofu into the air fryer and shut the lid. Cook for 10 minutes until golden and crispy.
6. Serve the tofu satay while hot, topped with chopped roasted peanuts.

Air Fryer Spicy Chicken Burgers

MAKES 4 SERVINGS
PREPARATION TIME - 5 MINUTES
COOKING TIME - 15 MINUTES
NUTRITIONAL VALUES PER SERVING - 290 KCALS, 15 G CARBS, 22 G PROTEIN, 9 G FAT

INGREDIENTS

- ◆ 400 g chicken breast fillets, boneless and skinless
- ◆ ½ white onion, peeled and finely sliced
- ◆ 1 tsp Cajun seasoning
- ◆ 1 tsp chili powder
- ◆ 1 tsp garlic powder
- ◆ 2 tbsp dried mixed herbs
- ◆ 1 tsp salt
- ◆ 1 tsp black pepper
- ◆ 1 egg, beaten
- ◆ 1 tbsp soy sauce

METHOD

1. Line the bottom of the air fryer basket with greaseproof paper.
2. Chop the chicken breast into pieces and place in a large mixing bowl.
3. Add the finely sliced onion, Cajun seasoning, chili powder, garlic powder, dried mixed herbs, salt, and black pepper to the bowl, and stir well to fully combine the ingredients.
4. Whisk the eggs and soy sauce together in a separate bowl and pour into the bowl with the chicken and spice mixture.
5. Shape the mixture into 4 even patties. Transfer the patties into the prepared air fryer basket and cook for 15 minutes, turning halfway through. The chicken should be fully cooked and the burgers should be slightly crispy on the edges after the total cooking time.
6. Serve the burgers in a burger bun with a sauce of your choice and a side salad.

Air Fryer Chili Con Carne or Non Carne

MAKES 4 SERVINGS
PREPARATION TIME - 15 MINUTES
COOKING TIME - 20 MINUTES
NUTRITIONAL VALUE PER SERVING - 411 KCALS, 27G CARBS, 30G PROTEIN, 19G FAT

INGREDIENTS

- 3 tbsp olive oil
- 400 g beef mince or soy mince
- 1 white onion, finely chopped
- 1 red pepper, sliced
- 2 cloves garlic, peeled and finely grated
- 2 tsp chili powder
- 2 tsp ground cumin
- 2 tsp smoked paprika
- 2 tsp dried mixed herbs
- 1 tsp salt
- 1 tsp black pepper
- 4 tbsp tomato purée
- 1 x 400 g can of chopped tomatoes
- 4 x beef stock cubes or vegetable stock cubes
- 1 x 400 g can black beans, drained and rinsed
- 200 g white or brown rice, dry and uncooked

METHOD

1. Heat 2 tbsp olive oil in a large frying pan and add the beef or soy mince. Fry over a high heat for 10-12 minutes until evenly browned.
2. Transfer the beef mince or soy mince to the air fryer.
3. Heat the remaining 1 tbsp olive oil in the frying pan and add the white onion, red pepper, and garlic cloves. Cook for 7-8 minutes until the vegetables begin to soften.
4. Add the chili powder, ground cumin, smoked paprika, dried mixed herbs, salt, and black pepper to the pan. Cook for a further 2 minutes.
5. Line the air fryer basket with greaseproof paper.
6. Stir the tomato puree into the pan and transfer the mixture to the air fryer. Pour in the chopped tomatoes and mix well.
7. Boil a kettle of water and use it to dissolve the 4 beef stock cubes or vegetable stock cubes if you're making chili non carne. Pour the stock into the air fryer and stir well.
8. Turn the air fryer to 180 degrees Celsius, close the lid, and cook the chili for 10 minutes.
9. After 10 minutes, add the black beans to the air fryer and continue cooking the chili for another 10 minutes.
10. Meanwhile, cook the rice according to the packet instructions. Once cooked, spread the rice evenly across four bowls.
11. When the chili is ready, serve it on top of the beds of rice. Add a side of sour cream and tortilla chips for a delicious dinner.

Air Fryer Hunter's Chicken

MAKES 4 SERVINGS
PREPARATION TIME - 15 MINUTES
COOKING TIME - 10 MINUTES
NUTRITIONAL VALUES PER SERVING - 324 KCALS, 19 G CARBS, 24 G PROTEIN, 11 G FAT

INGREDIENTS

- 500 g potatoes, cut into 1 cm thick slices
- 2 tbsp oil
- 4 rashers smoke bacon

- 4 x 160 g skinless, boneless chicken breast fillets
- 50 g cheddar cheese, grated
- 4 tbsp BBQ sauce
- 1 tsp black pepper

METHOD

1. Preheat the air fryer to 200 degrees Celsius and line the bottom of the basket with parchment paper.
2. Place the cut potatoes in a bowl of cold water for 30 minutes to remove any excess starch. Drain well and pat dry with a paper towel.
3. Add the potatoes to a bowl and toss in 2 tbsp olive oil. Set aside.
4. Wrap with bacon around the chicken breasts. Secure in place with a cocktail stick and transfer to the air fryer. Add the potatoes to the air fryer.
5. Close the lid and cook the chicken and potatoes for 10 minutes.
6. After 10 minutes, open the lid of the air fryer and sprinkle the cheddar cheese over the top of each chicken breast. Shut the lid again and cook for a further 10 minutes.
7. Once cooked, remove the chicken breasts and serve with BBQ sauce and a sprinkle of black pepper.

Air Fryer Vegan Veggie-Filled Lasagne

MAKES 4 SERVINGS
PREPARATION TIME - 15 MINUTES
COOKING TIME - 25 MINUTES
NUTRITIONAL VALUE PER SERVING - 654 KCALS, 43G CARBS, 34G PROTEIN, 28G FAT

INGREDIENTS

- 2 tbsp olive oil
- 1 white onion, sliced
- 1 clove garlic, peeled and crushed
- 2 courgettes, diced
- 1 carrot, diced
- 1 red pepper, deseeded and cut into chunks
- 400 g meat-free chicken style pieces (such as Quorn pieces)
- 1 x 400 g jar of Alfredo sauce
- 1 x 400 g can of chopped tomatoes
- 3 tbsp tomato paste
- 8 sheets lasagne
- 50 g vegan cheese, grated

METHOD

1. Line the air fryer basket with greaseproof paper or olive oil.
2. Heat 1 tbsp of olive oil in a large frying pan and add the onion slices and crushed garlic. Cook for 8-10 minutes until they start to soften and become fragrant.
3. Add the courgettes, carrots, and red pepper, and cook for a further 2-3 minutes to slightly soften the vegetables but not fully cook them.
4. Transfer the vegetables to a bowl and set aside.
5. Heat the remaining 1 tbsp olive oil in the frying pan and add the meat-free chicken style pieces. Cook for 8-10 minutes until slightly golden on each side.

6. Transfer the meat-free chicken style pieces to the same bowl as the cooked vegetables.
7. Spread a layer of Alfredo sauce along the bottom of the lined air fryer basket using a quarter of the total amount of sauce.
8. On top of the Alfredo sauce, spread a quarter of the vegetable and meat-free chicken style pieces mixture.
9. Layer 2 lasagne sheets on top, followed by a third of the can of chopped tomatoes and 1 tbsp tomato paste.
10. Repeat steps 7 to 9 until all of the ingredients have been used. The final layer should comprise 2 lasagne sheets.
11. Close the lid of the air fryer and turn it to a heat setting around 180 degrees Celsius. Cook for 20 minutes until the lasagne sheets are well-cooked and the vegetables are soft.
12. Open the lid of the air fryer and sprinkle the grated vegan cheese on top of the lasagne sheets.
13. Close the air fryer lid once again and continue cooking the lasagne for a further 5 minutes until the cheese has melted.
14. Serve the lasagne with a side of your choice.

Air Fryer Chicken and Veggie Pasta

MAKES 4 SERVINGS
PREPARATION TIME - 15 MINUTES
COOKING TIME - 15 MINUTES
NUTRITIONAL VALUE PER SERVING - 301 KCALS, 30 G CARBS, 28 G PROTEIN, 7 G FAT

INGREDIENTS

- 400 g skinless, boneless chicken breast, sliced
- 1 white onion, peeled and sliced
- 1 stick celery, sliced
- 1 red pepper, deseeded and sliced
- 1 tsp dried mixed herbs
- 1 tsp black pepper
- 1 tsp salt
- 4 nests of pasta, dry and uncooked

METHOD

1. Place the chicken, white onion, celery, and red pepper in a bowl. Add the dried mixed herbs, black pepper, and salt.
2. Transfer to the air fryer and cook at 200 degrees Celsius for 15 minutes until the chicken is browned and the vegetables are soft.
3. Just before the air fryer is due to finish, bring a pan of water to a boil and add the pasta. Once boiling, lower the heat to a gentle simmer and add a sprinkle of salt to the pan.
4. Cook the pasta for 10 minutes until soft.
5. Serve the pasta evenly between 4 dishes and top with the chicken and vegetable mixture. Add grated cheese and an extra sprinkle of black pepper for some additional flavour!

Air Fryer Chicken Tikka Masala

MAKES 4 SERVINGS
PREPARATION TIME - 20 MINUTES
COOKING TIME - 20 MINUTES
NUTRITIONAL VALUE PER SERVING - 452 KCALS, 31 G CARBS, 36 G PROTEIN, 15 G FAT

INGREDIENTS

- 1 tbsp olive oil

- 1 tsp cumin seeds

- 1 tbsp garam masala

- 1 tbsp curry powder

- 1 tsp black pepper

- 1 white onion, finely sliced

- 2 cloves garlic, peeled and crushed

- 1 red pepper, finely sliced

- 1 red chili pepper, finely sliced

- 2 tbsp tomato paste

- 1 x 400 g can of chopped tomatoes

- 1 x 400 g boneless, skinless chicken breast, diced

- 1 tbsp dried coriander

METHOD

1. Heat 1 tbsp olive oil in a large wok or frying pan and add the cumin seeds.

2. Cook for 1-2 minutes before adding the garam masala, curry powder, and black pepper to the pan. Cook for a further 2 minutes until you can begin to smell the spices.

3. Add the white onion, garlic, red pepper, chili pepper, and tomato paste to the frying pan, and cook for a further 2 minutes.

4. Coat the basket of the air fryer with olive oil or cover it with greaseproof paper.

5. Transfer the ingredients from the pan to the lined air fryer tray, pour the chopped tomatoes in, and give it a stir.

6. Add the diced chicken breast and 1 tbsp dried coriander.

7. Close the lid of the air fryer and turn it to a medium heat setting. Cook the chicken tikka masala for 20 minutes until the ingredients are well-cooked, and the dish is hot.

8. Serve with a side of pilau rice, poppadoms, naan bread, and mango chutney.

Air Fryer Chicken Satay

MAKES 4 SERVINGS
PREPARATION TIME - 20 MINUTES
COOKING TIME - 10 MINUTES
NUTRITIONAL VALUES PER SERVING - 356 KCALS, 14 G CARBS, 23 G PROTEIN, 12 G FAT

INGREDIENTS

- 400 g skinless, boneless chicken breast fillets, cubed
- 3 tbsp soy sauce
- 2 tbsp hot sauce
- 2 tbsp brown sugar
- 1 tsp garlic powder
- 2 tsp ground cumin
- 50 g roasted peanuts, chopped

METHOD

1. Preheat the air fryer to 200 degrees Celsius and line the bottom of the basket with parchment paper.
2. Place the chicken cubes in a bowl.
3. In a separate bowl, whisk the soy sauce, hot sauce, brown sugar, garlic powder, and ground cumin together until fully combined.
4. Toss the chicken breast cubes until fully coated in the sauce. Place back in the bowl and cover with clingfilm. Leave the chicken to marinate for 10 minutes.
5. Transfer the coated chicken chunks to the air fryer. Shut the lid and cook for 12-15 minutes until the chicken is well-cooked and fragrant.
6. Serve the chicken breast chunks while still hot with sides of your choice and the chopped peanuts sprinkled on top.

Sticky Air Fryer Tofu With Egg Fried Rice

MAKES 4 SERVINGS
PREPARATION TIME - 10 MINUTES
COOKING TIME - 15 MINUTES
NUTRITIONAL VALUES PER SERVING - 345 KCALS, 22 G CARBS, 22 G PROTEIN, 11 G FAT

INGREDIENTS

- 1 x 400 g firm tofu
- 400 g cooked white or brown rice
- 100 g fresh or canned peas and sweetcorn
- 2 tbsp olive oil
- 2 eggs, beaten

METHOD

1. Line the air fryer basket with greaseproof paper.
2. Cut the tofu into chunks and add to the air fryer basket.
3. Shut the lid, turn the air fryer onto 180 degrees Celsius, and cook the tofu for 5 minutes.
4. Once the tofu is cooked, turn the air fryer onto a low heat and leave the tofu in the basket while you create the egg fried rice.
5. In a bowl, mix the cooked white or brown rice and the fresh peas and sweetcorn.
6. Add the tbsp olive oil and toss to coat the rice evenly. Whisk in the eggs.
7. Transfer the egg rice to the air fryer basket, close the lid, and cook for 15 minutes until the eggs are cooked, the rice is soft, and the tofu is crispy.
8. Serve for dinner with a sauce of your choice and some extra vegetables.

SWEET TREATS

When you're craving a sweet treat after dinner or you want a mid-afternoon snack, you'll love all of the recipes that we have got for you to finish up this air fryer cookbook. Keep reading to learn how to make lots of delicious desserts and snacks.

Crunchy Air Fryer Peanut Cookies

MAKES 12 SERVINGS
PREPARATION TIME - 10 MINUTES
COOKING TIME - 10 MINUTES
NUTRITIONAL VALUES PER SERVING - 145 CALORIES, 15
G CARBOHYDRATES, 9 G FAT, 3 G PROTEIN

INGREDIENTS

- 100 g flour
- 8 tbsp smooth peanut butter
- 100 g peanuts
- 100 g granulated sugar
- 8 tbsp butter
- 1 egg
- ½ tsp salt

METHOD

1. Line the air fryer basket with greaseproof paper.
2. Add the flour, peanut butter, and peanuts into a bowl. Fold in the granulated sugar and butter.
3. Whisk the egg into the bowl and add a sprinkle of salt.
4. Shape the dough into 12 even cookies and place in the lined air fryer basket.
5. Shut the lid and cook on 180 degrees Celsius for 10 minutes until golden and crunchy.

Air Fryer Doughnuts

MAKES 4 SERVINGS
PREPARATION TIME - 1 HOUR 30 MINUTES
COOKING TIME - 10 MINUTES
NUTRITIONAL VALUES PER SERVING - 275 CALORIES, 45
G CARBOHYDRATES, 8 G FAT, 4 G PROTEIN

INGREDIENTS

FOR THE DOUGHNUTS:

- 150 ml milk (any type)
- 50 g butter, unsalted and slightly melted to a lukewarm temperature
- 1 x 7 g sachet of dried fast-action yeast
- 60 g caster sugar
- 2 tsp vanilla extract
- 300 g plain flour
- 1 tsp ground cinnamon
- 1 egg, beaten

FOR THE GLAZE:

- 125 g icing sugar
- 3 tbsp milk

METHOD

1. Start preparing the doughnuts by combining the milk, melted salted butter, yeast, caster sugar, and 1 tsp vanilla extract in a bowl.
2. Stir well to fully combine into one smooth mixture and set aside for 20 minutes to allow the yeast to foam.
3. Meanwhile, combine the plain flour, remaining 1 tsp of vanilla extract, cinnamon, and beaten egg in a separate bowl. Fold this mixture into the dry mixture and mix well.
4. Knead the dough for 8-10 minutes until tacky. Cover the bowl with a clean tea towel and leave to rise for an hour. The dough should double in size.
5. Sprinkle some flour on a clean surface and roll out the dough to around 1.5 cm thick.
6. Use two doughnut cutters, one larger and one smaller, to create doughnuts from the rolled-out dough.
7. Place the doughnuts carefully onto a lined baking tray and transfer them to the air fryer.
8. Shut the lid of the switch the machine onto a medium heat setting or around 180 degrees Celsius. Cook the doughnuts for 8-10 minutes until golden and hot.
9. While the doughnuts are cooking, make the glaze by combining the icing sugar and milk in a small bowl.
10. Once the doughnuts are cooked, gently brush the glaze on top of each one and leave them to dry on a wire rack.
11. The doughnuts are best eaten on the same day while they're still fresh. However, they will keep for up to a day as long as they're stored in an airtight container.

Air Fryer Apple Fritters with Apple Cider Glaze

MAKES 12 SERVINGS
PREPARATION TIME - 20 MINUTES
COOKING TIME - 10 MINUTES
NUTRITIONAL VALUES PER SERVING - 232 CALORIES, 35
G CARBOHYDRATES, 5 G FAT, 3 G PROTEIN

INGREDIENTS

FOR THE APPLE FRITTERS:

- 2 large apples
- 500 g plain flour
- 100 g granulated sugar
- 1 tbsp baking powder
- 1 tsp salt
- 1 tsp cinnamon
- 1 tsp nutmeg

- 100 ml apple cider or apple juice
- 2 eggs, beaten
- 3 tbsp butter, melted
- 1 tsp vanilla extract
- Oil

FOR THE APPLE CIDER GLAZE:

- 100 g powdered sugar
- 50 ml apple cider or apple juice
- 1 tsp cinnamon

METHOD

1. Peel and core the apples, and chop them into small chunks. Lay the apple pieces out on a kitchen towel and pat any excess moisture away.

2. In a large mixing bowl, combine the flour, sugar, baking powder, salt, cinnamon, and nutmeg. Add the flour and toss to coat in the flour mixture.

3. In a separate bowl, whisk together the apple cider, beaten eggs, melted butter, and vanilla extract. Stir the wet mixture into the dry mixture.

4. Preheat the air fryer to around 200 degrees Celsius. Cover the bottom of the air fryer basket with greaseproof paper.

5. Scoop small dollops of the dough into the air fryer and lightly spray with oil.

6. Shut the lid of the air fryer and cook the apple fritters for 8-10 minutes until golden and crispy.

7. While the fritters are cooking in the air fryer, make the glaze by combining the three ingredients in a bowl.

8. Drizzle the glaze over the apple fritters when they're ready and leave them to set for 10 minutes before serving.

Air Fryer Oat and Fruit Muffins

MAKES 8 SERVINGS
PREPARATION TIME - 15 MINUTES
COOKING TIME - 10 MINUTES
NUTRITIONAL VALUES PER SERVING - 203 KCALS, 21 G CARBS, 11 G PROTEIN, 9 G FAT

INGREDIENTS

- ◆ 200 g classic rolled oats
- ◆ 200 g plain flour
- ◆ 2 tsp baking powder
- ◆ 100 g caster sugar
- ◆ 50 g raisins
- ◆ 50 g cranberries
- ◆ 1 egg, beaten
- ◆ 200 ml milk (any type)
- ◆ 1 tsp vanilla extract

METHOD

1. Grease an 8-pan muffin tray with olive oil and preheat the air fryer to 180 degrees Celsius.
2. In a bowl, combine the classic rolled oats, plain flour, baking powder, and caster sugar until fully mixed. Add the raisins and cranberries.
3. In another bowl, whisk together the beaten egg, milk, and vanilla extract.
4. Fold the dry mixture into the wet mixture and evenly spoon into the 8 muffin cases.
5. Transfer the muffin tray into the air fryer and close the lid. Cook for 10 minutes until golden on top and hot in the centre. You can test this by inserting a knife into the centre of the muffins. It should come out dry when the muffins are fully cooked.
6. Serve the muffins hot or cold. Store any leftovers in an airtight cake tin and consume within 5-7 days.

Air Fryer Banana and White Chocolate Loaf

MAKES 8 SERVINGS
PREPARATION TIME - 10 MINUTES
COOKING TIME - 1 HOUR 10 MINUTES
NUTRITIONAL VALUES PER SERVING - 245 KCALS, 20 G CARBS, 8 G PROTEIN, 14 G FAT

INGREDIENTS

- 250 g plain flour
- 1 tsp baking powder
- 1 tsp ground cinnamon
- 1 tsp ground nutmeg
- 1 tsp salt
- 2 ripe bananas, peeled
- 2 eggs, beaten
- 100 g granulated sugar
- 50 g brown sugar
- 100 g white chocolate, broken into pieces
- 4 tbsp oat milk
- 2 tbsp olive oil
- 1 tsp vanilla extract

METHOD

1. In a large mixing bowl, combine the plain flour, baking powder, ground cinnamon, ground nutmeg, and salt.
2. Mash the ripe bananas in a separate bowl until there are no lumps. Add the beaten eggs, granulated sugar, brown sugar, and white chocolate chips to the bowl and whisk until well combined.
3. Stir in the oat milk, olive oil, and vanilla extract. Combine the dry and wet ingredients and whisk into one smooth mixture.
4. Pour the batter into the lined loaf tin and carefully transfer it into the air fryer basket.
5. Close the lid of the air fryer and cook the banana and white chocolate chip loaf for 30 minutes until the cake is set and golden on top
6. Insert a knife into the centre of the cake. It should come out dry when the cake is fully cooked.
7. Remove the loaf tin from the air fryer and set it aside to cool on a drying rack for at least 20 minutes before cutting into slices.
8. Enjoy the cake hot or cold and store leftovers in an airtight tin.

Air Fryer Black Bean Brownies

MAKES 8 SERVINGS
PREPARATION TIME - 15 MINUTES
COOKING TIME - 15 MINUTES
NUTRITIONAL VALUE PER SERVING - 189 KCALS, 17 G CARBS, 12 G PROTEIN, 5 G FAT

INGREDIENTS

- 400 g plain flour
- ½ tsp baking powder
- 4 tbsp cocoa powder
- 8 tbsp butter
- 50 g milk chocolate, broken into pieces
- 50 g dark chocolate, broken into pieces
- 100 g granulated sugar
- 400 g dried black beans
- 100 g dried fruit of any kind (raisins, sultanas, or cranberries)
- 3 eggs, beaten
- 1 tsp vanilla extract
- ½ tsp salt

METHOD

1. Cover a rectangular brownie tin with greaseproof paper.
2. In a bowl, whisk together the flour, baking powder, and cocoa powder until well combined.
3. In a large heatproof bowl, place the butter, milk chocolate, and dark. Place the bowl above a pan of simmering water. Warm the mixture over a gentle heat until melted.
4. Remove the bowl from the heat and pour the sugar into the butter and chocolate mixture. Whisk in the eggs, vanilla, and salt.
5. Fold the black beans and raisins into the bowl and mix well.
6. Whisk in the eggs, vanilla, and salt.
7. Stir the flour mixture into the pan until fully combined. Transfer the brownie mixture into a lined brownie tin and place in the air fryer. Even out the top layer of the mixture using the back of a spoon so that it is smooth.
8. Close the lid of the air fryer and turn it to 180 degrees Celsius.
9. Cook for 15 minutes until the top of the brownie is set, and the inside is hot and gooey.
10. Once cooked, remove the brownie tray from the air fryer and leave it to cool on a drying rack.
11. Serve the brownie hot or cold with a side of ice cream or whipped cream. Store any leftovers in the fridge for no more than 5 days.

Air Fryer Peanut Butter Clusters

MAKES 20 SERVINGS
PREPARATION TIME - 5 MINUTES
COOKING TIME - 5 MINUTES
NUTRITIONAL VALUE PER SERVING - 366 KCALS, 28 G CARBS, 9 G PROTEIN, 12 G FAT

INGREDIENTS

- 400 g salted, dry roasted peanuts
- 100 g milk chocolate chips
- 100 g white chocolate chips
- 50 g dried cranberries
- 50 g raisins
- 2 tbsp peanut butter powder
- 8 tbsp peanut butter

METHOD

1. In a large mixing bowl, combine the peanuts, milk chocolate chips, white chocolate chips, dried cranberries, raisins, and peanut butter powder. Use a large spoon to stir the ingredients together.

2. Stir in the peanut butter and mix well to fully coat all of the ingredients in the bowl.

3. Scoop the mixture into small, even clusters, and place into the air fryer.

4. Shut the lid of the air fryer and cook the peanut butter clusters for 5 minutes until crispy and golden.

5. Eat the clusters as a snack or for dessert and store any leftovers in the fridge for a maximum of 5 days.

Air Fryer Strawberry Cake

MAKES 8 SERVINGS
PREPARATION TIME - 15 MINUTES
COOKING TIME - 15 MINUTES
NUTRITIONAL VALUE PER SERVING - 143 KCALS, 17 G CARBS, 4 G PROTEIN, 12 G FAT

INGREDIENTS

- 200 g plain white flour
- 1 tsp baking powder
- 1 tbsp chia seeds
- 200 g fresh strawberries, chopped
- 2 eggs, beaten
- 4 tbsp honey
- 200 ml oat milk
- 2 tsp vanilla extract

METHOD

1. Grease a loaf tin with olive oil or butter, or line it with parchment paper.
2. In a bowl, whisk together the plain white flour, baking powder, and chia seeds.
3. Stir in the strawberries, beaten eggs, and honey.
4. Stir in the oat milk and vanilla extract.
5. Pour the batter into the lined loaf tin and place it in the air fryer.
6. Shut the lid and turn the machine to 180 degrees Celsius. Cook the cake for 15 minutes. Once cooked, the cake should be golden on top. Insert a knife into the centre of the cake and it will come out dry when the cake is ready.
7. Serve immediately or leave to cool on a drying rack. Store any leftovers in an airtight loaf tin for no more than 5 days.

Air Fryer Date, Chia Seed, and Peanut Butter Bites

MAKES 15 SERVINGS
PREPARATION TIME - 10 MINUTES
COOKING TIME - 10 MINUTES
NUTRITIONAL VALUE PER SERVING - 178 KCALS, 15 G CARBS, 4 G PROTEIN, 12 G FAT

INGREDIENTS

- 400 g pitted dates
- 8 tbsp chia seeds
- 8 tbsp smooth peanut butter
- 100 g dark chocolate, broken into pieces
- 2 tbsp agave syrup

METHOD

1. Place the pitted dates, chia seeds, peanut butter, milk chocolate, and agave syrup in a blender.
2. Pulse in 10-second intervals until the ingredients are well mixed and form a homogenous mixture.
3. Scoop the mixture out in spoonfuls and shape them into even balls.
4. Place the balls into the air fry basket and close the lid. Cook the date balls for 10 minutes.
5. Remove the balls from the air fryer and leave them to set in the refrigerator. Store in the fridge for a maximum of 5 days.

Air Fryer Banana, Caramel, and Walnut Cake

MAKES 8 SERVINGS
PREPARATION TIME - 10 MINUTES
COOKING TIME - 15 MINUTES
NUTRITIONAL VALUE PER SERVING - 438 KCALS, 35 G CARBS, 10 G PROTEIN, 29 G FAT

INGREDIENTS

- 1 x 400 g can of condensed milk
- 200 g plain flour
- 100 g granulated sugar
- 1 tsp baking powder
- 2 bananas, mashed
- 2 eggs, beaten
- 200 ml cashew milk
- 2 tbsp coconut oil
- 1 tsp vanilla extract
- 4 tbsp walnuts, chopped
- 100 ml double cream

METHOD

1. Remove the label from the can of condensed milk can and place it in a pan. Fill the pan with around 2 inches of water so that the water comes up to around a third of the way up the can.
2. Bring the water to a boil, then lower it to a gentle simmer. Leave the condensed milk to cook for around 3 hours to caramelise the milk.
3. Meanwhile, line a loaf tin with greaseproof paper.
4. In a large mixing bowl, whisk together the flour, granulated sugar, and baking powder.
5. In a separate bowl, combine the mashed bananas, beaten eggs, milk, coconut oil, and vanilla extract.
6. Combine the dry and wet mixtures and mix well until a smooth cake batter forms.
7. Stir the walnuts into the batter, followed by the double cream. Finally, stir in the now-caramelised milk.
8. Carefully pour the cake batter into the lined loaf tin and transfer it into the air fryer basket.
9. Cook the cake at 180 degrees Celsius for 15 minutes until golden on top. Insert a knife into the middle of the cake and it should come out dry when the cake is ready.
10. Allow the cake to cool on a drying rack before serving. Store any leftovers in an airtight cake tin for a maximum of 5 days.

Air Fryer Vegan Triple Chocolate Fudge

MAKES 8 SERVINGS
PREPARATION TIME - 10 MINUTES
COOKING TIME - 10 MINUTES
NUTRITIONAL VALUE PER SERVING - 344 KCALS, 28 G CARBS, 12 G PROTEIN, 19 G FAT

INGREDIENTS

- 200 g plain flour
- 100 g granulated sugar
- 2 tbsp cocoa powder
- 1 tsp baking powder
- ½ tsp salt
- 200 ml soy milk or oat milk
- 1 tsp vanilla extract
- 100 g vegan milk chocolate chips
- 100 g vegan white chocolate chips
- 100 g vegan dark chocolate chips

METHOD

1. In a bowl, add the flour, granulated sugar, cocoa powder, baking powder, and salt. Stir until fully combined.
2. Fold in the soy or oat milk and vanilla extract. Add the milk chocolate chips, white chocolate chips, and dark chocolate chips. Stir well to fully combine.
3. Pour the mixture into a lined brownie tray and place in the air fryer and use a spoon to spread the top of the fudge into an even layer.
4. Close the lid on the air fryer and cook the fudge for 10 minutes at 180 degrees Celsius.
5. Leave the fudge to cool on a drying rack and serve hot or cold. Store any leftovers in the fridge for no more than 5 days.

Air Fryer Orange and Chia Seed Muffins

MAKES 8 SERVINGS
PREPARATION TIME - 10 MINUTES
COOKING TIME - 25 MINUTES
NUTRITIONAL VALUES PER SERVING - 112 KCALS, 9 G CARBS, 4 G PROTEIN, 7 G FAT

INGREDIENTS

- 200 g plain flour

- 1 tsp baking powder

- 100 g granulated sugar

- 1 tsp ground cinnamon

- 1 tsp ground nutmeg

- Peel and zest 1 orange

- 4 tbsp chia seeds

- 2 eggs, beaten

- 100 ml milk

- 50 ml orange juice

- 1 tsp vanilla extract

METHOD

1. Preheat the air fryer to 150 degrees Celsius and line an 8-pan muffin tin with cases.
2. In a large mixing bowl, whisk together the plain flour, baking powder, granulated sugar, ground cinnamon, ground nutmeg, orange peel and zest, and chia seeds.
3. Whisk the beaten eggs, milk, orange juice, and vanilla extract. Stir until well combined.
4. Fold the dry ingredients into the wet ingredients and mix well.
5. Evenly spread the cake batter into the 8 muffin cases and carefully place in the air fryer basket.
6. Shut the lid and cook the muffins for 25 minutes until they are golden and cooked all the way through. You can insert a knife into the centre of each one and it will be dry if they are ready.
7. Set the muffins aside to cool on a drying rack before serving. Store leftovers in an airtight bread tin.

Air Fryer Chocolate and Strawberry Pastry Puffs

MAKES 8 SERVINGS
PREPARATION TIME - 20 MINUTES
COOKING TIME - 10 MINUTES
NUTRITIONAL VALUES PER SERVING - 245 KCALS, 25 G CARBS, 6 G PROTEIN, 16 G FAT

INGREDIENTS

FOR THE FILLING:

- 100 g fresh strawberries
- 100 g milk chocolate chips
- 50 g granulated sugar
- 50 g granulated sugar
- 1 tsp corn starch

FOR THE PASTRY:

- 1 sheet pre-made puff pastry

FOR THE FROSTING:

- 4 tbsp powdered sugar
- 2 tbsp maple syrup

METHOD

1. Preheat the air fryer to 180 degrees Celsius and line the mesh basket with parchment paper.
2. To create the filling, combine the strawberries, milk chocolate chips, granulated sugar, and brown sugar in a bowl. Transfer to a saucepan and place over medium heat.
3. Gently heat the mixture until it begins to boil. Lower the temperature and continue heating until it forms a smooth mixture.

4. Whisk the corn starch into the pan and simmer for 2-3 minutes. Remove the saucepan from the heat and set it aside to cool while you prepare the puff pastry.

5. To prepare the pastry, roll the large sheet of puff pastry onto a clean surface. Cut the pastry into 8 equal rectangles.

6. Carefully spoon 2 tbsp of the strawberry and chocolate filling onto one side of each of the puff pastry rectangles.

7. Fold the plain side of each puff pastry rectangle to seal the filings inside. Press the sides down with a fork or your fingers to keep the fillings fully covered during the cooking process.

8. Transfer the puff pastry rectangles into the prepared air fryer basket and cook for 8-10 minutes until the pastry is slightly risen and has become golden and crispy.

9. While the puff pastry tarts are cooking in the air fryer, prepare the frosting by whisking together the powdered sugar and maple syrup in a small bowl.

10. When the puff pastry sheets are cooked, remove then from the air fryer and set aside to cool for a short while.

11. Once cooled, spread a light layer of frosting onto one side of each of the puff pastry tarts. Leave to set.

12. Serve hot or cold and store any leftover puff pastry tarts in the fridge for no more than five days.

Air Fryer Chocolate Souffle

MAKES 2 SERVINGS
PREPARATION TIME - 15 MINUTES
COOKING TIME - 15 MINUTES
NUTRITIONAL VALUES PER SERVING - 299 KCALS, 28 G CARBS, 10 G PROTEIN, 18 G FAT

INGREDIENTS

- 100 g milk chocolate
- 100 g dark chocolate
- 100 g brown sugar
- 4 tbsp oat or cashew milk
- ½ tsp vanilla extract
- 4 egg whites, plus two egg yolks

METHOD

1. Preheat the air fryer to 180 degrees Celsius and line the mesh basket with parchment paper or grease it with olive oil.
2. Place the two types of chocolate in a bowl. Lay the bowl over a saucepan of hot water and gently heat until the chocolate melts. Stir it frequently to prevent it from burning.
3. Remove the bowl from the heat. Stir the brown sugar, milk, and vanilla extract.
4. Whisk the egg whites and egg yolks in a bowl until well combined.
5. Fold a third of the eggs into the chocolate mixture and stir until it forms a smooth and consistent mixture.
6. Repeat step 5 another two times with the other two-thirds of the eggs.
7. Pour the chocolate souffle mixture evenly into two ramekins and place them in the lined air fryer basket.
8. Cook the chocolate souffles for a total of 15 minutes until hot and set on top.

Air Fry Vegan Chocolate and Banana Loaf

MAKES 8 SERVINGS
PREPARATION TIME - 10 MINUTES
COOKING TIME - 40 MINUTES
NUTRITIONAL VALUES PER SERVING - 165 KCALS, 19 G CARBS, 8 G PROTEIN, 12 G FAT

INGREDIENTS

- 400 g plain flour
- 1 tsp baking powder
- 100 g brown sugar
- 1 tsp ground cinnamon
- ½ tsp salt
- 2 ripe bananas, peeled
- 2 eggs, beaten
- 100 g vegan milk chocolate chips
- 100 g dark chocolate chips
- 8 tbsp oat milk
- 2 tbsp olive oil
- 1 tsp vanilla extract

METHOD

1. Preheat the air fryer to 150 degrees Celsius and line a loaf tin with parchment paper.
2. In a large mixing bowl, combine the plain flour, baking powder, brown sugar, ground cinnamon, and salt.
3. Mash the ripe bananas in a separate bowl until it is lump-free.
4. Whisk the beaten eggs into the bowl.
5. Stir in the vegan chocolate chips, dark chocolate chips, oar milk, olive oil, and vanilla extract. Fold the ingredients until they create a smooth mixture.
6. Pour the cake batter into the prepared loaf tin and transfer into the air fryer basket.
7. Cook the cake for 40 minutes until it is golden on top. Insert a sharp knife into the centre of the cake and when it's ready, the knife will come out dry.
8. Remove the loaf tin from the air fryer and set aside to cool on a drying rack for 20 minutes.
9. Once the cake has cooled, cut it into slices and serve. Store any leftovers in an airtight loaf tin for no more than five days.

Air Fryer Dough Balls With Chocolate Frosting

MAKES 8 SERVINGS
PREPARATION TIME - 1 HOUR 10 MINUTES
COOKING TIME - 5 MINUTES
NUTRITIONAL VALUES PER SERVING - 234 KCALS, 23 G CARBS, 9 G PROTEIN, 15 G FAT

INGREDIENTS

FOR THE DONUTS:

- 200 ml milk (any kind)
- 100 g granulated sugar
- 1 tbsp active dry yeast
- 2 tbsp olive oil
- 4 tbsp butter, melted
- 1 egg, beaten
- 1 tsp vanilla extract
- 400 g / 14 oz plain flour
- 4 tbsp cocoa powder
- 1 tsp cinnamon

FOR THE FROSTING:

- 5 tbsp powdered sugar
- 2 tbsp cocoa powder
- 100 ml single cream
- 50 g chocolate spread

METHOD

1. To make the donuts, whisk the milk, granulated sugars, and active dry yeast in a bowl. Set aside for a few minutes in a warm environment while the yeast starts to get foamy.

2. Pour the melted butter, beaten egg, and vanilla extract into the bowl. Whisk until all of the ingredients are well combined.

3. Fold in the dry ingredients (the plain flour, cocoa powder, and cinnamon) until they create a smooth, consistent mixture.

4. Lightly flour a clean surface in your kitchen and roll the dough out.
5. Knead the dough for a few minutes until it becomes soft and sticky.
6. Transfer the dough into a large bowl and cover it with a clean tea towel. Set aside in a warm place for the dough to rise for one hour.
7. Remove the tea towel or tinfoil from the bowl and place on a floured surface once. Roll the dough into even balls about one inch in diameter.
8. Place the balls into a lined air fryer basket. Turn the machine onto 180 degrees Celsius and close the lid.
9. Cook the dough balls for 5-6 minutes until they are slightly golden.
10. While the dough balls are heating in the air fryer, make the frosting. Combine the powdered sugar, cocoa powder, single cream, and chocolate spread in a bowl. Mix well to create a smooth, sticky mixture.
11. When cooked, remove the dough balls from the air fryer. Set aside to cool for 10 minutes.
12. Once the dough balls have cooled, use a spoon to coat each one in frosting. Place in the fridge to allow the frosting to set for at least one hour.
13. Enjoy the dough balls hot or cold. Store your leftovers in the fridge for up to five days.

Dark Chocolate and Berry Cake

MAKES 8 SERVINGS
PREPARATION TIME - 10 MINUTES
COOKING TIME - 40 MINUTES
NUTRITIONAL VALUES PER SERVING - 213 KCALS, 17 G CARBS, 5 G PROTEIN, 11 G FAT

INGREDIENTS

- 400 g plain flour
- 1 tsp baking powder
- 1 tsp ground cinnamon
- 3 eggs, beaten
- 100 g granulated sugar
- 100 g dark chocolate, broken into pieces
- 100 g fresh raspberries
- 50 g fresh strawberries
- 50 g fresh blueberries
- 1 tbsp cocoa powder or cacao powder
- 4 tbsp milk (any kind)
- 1 tsp vanilla extract

METHOD

1. Preheat the air fryer to 180 degrees Celsius and line a cake tin with parchment paper.
2. In a large mixing bowl, combine the plain flour, baking powder, and ground cinnamon.
3. Whisk the eggs into the small bowl and stir in the granulated sugar. Mix well and fold these ingredients into the dry ingredients.
4. Stir in the dark chocolate chunks, as well as the fresh raspberries, strawberries, blueberries, milk, and vanilla extract.
5. Transfer the cake batter into a lined loaf tin. Place the loaf tin into the lined air fryer basket, close the lid, and cook for 40 minutes until the cake is golden and set in the centre.
6. Remove the cake from the air fryer, leaving it in the loaf tin. Set aside to cool on a drying rack before serving. Store leftovers in an airtight tin for up to five days.

EXCLUSIVE BONUS

40 Weight Loss Recipes

&

14 Days Meal Plan

Scan the QR-Code and receive
the FREE download:

Disclaimer

This book contains opinions and ideas of the author and is meant to teach the reader informative and helpful knowledge while due care should be taken by the user in the application of the information provided. The instructions and strategies are possibly not right for every reader and there is no guarantee that they work for everyone. Using this book and implementing the information/recipes therein contained is explicitly your own responsibility and risk. This work with all its contents, does not guarantee correctness, completion, quality or correctness of the provided information. Misinformation or misprints cannot be completely eliminated.

Printed in Great Britain
by Amazon

17628715R00080